High lights Frans Hals Museum

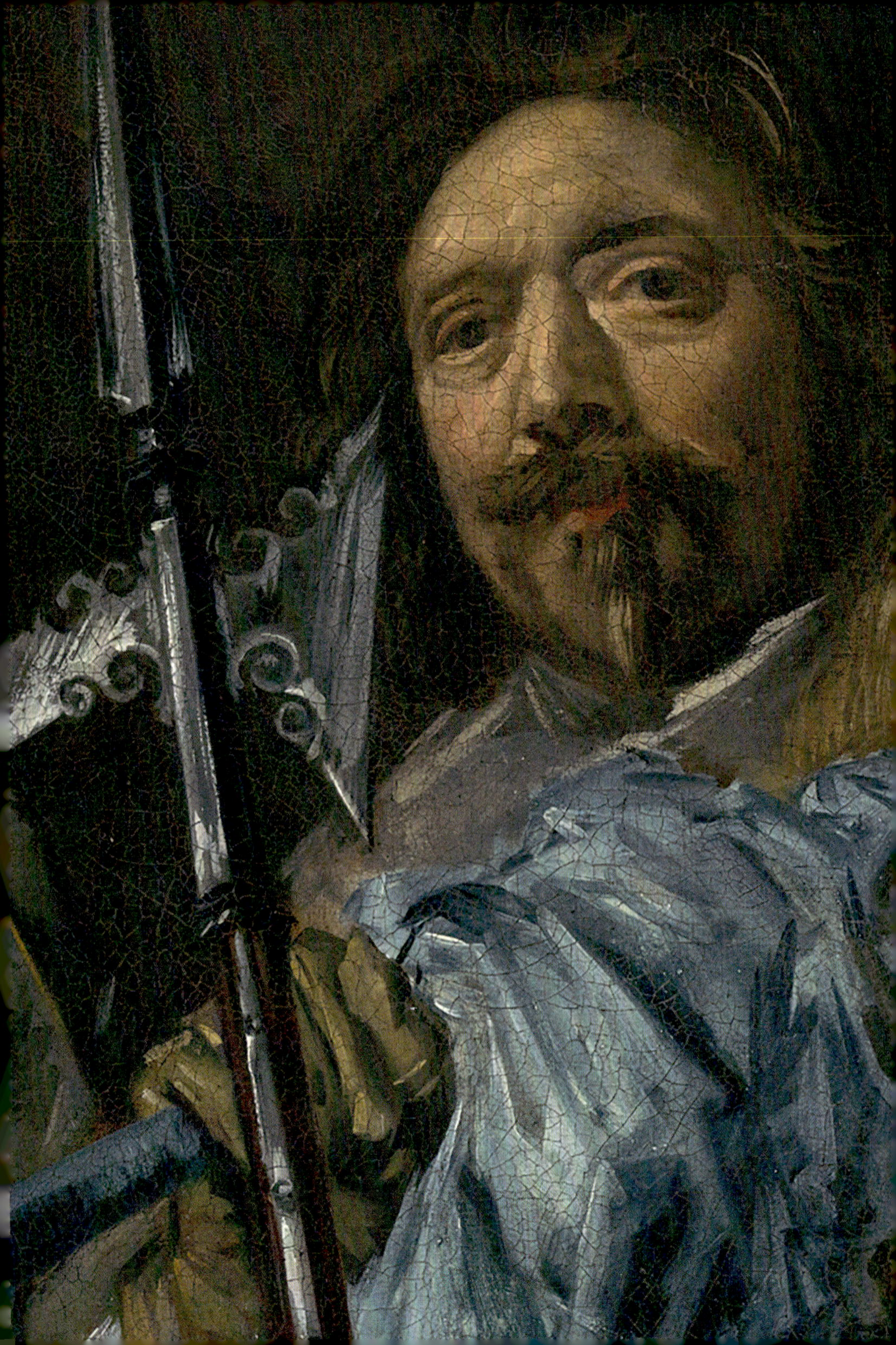

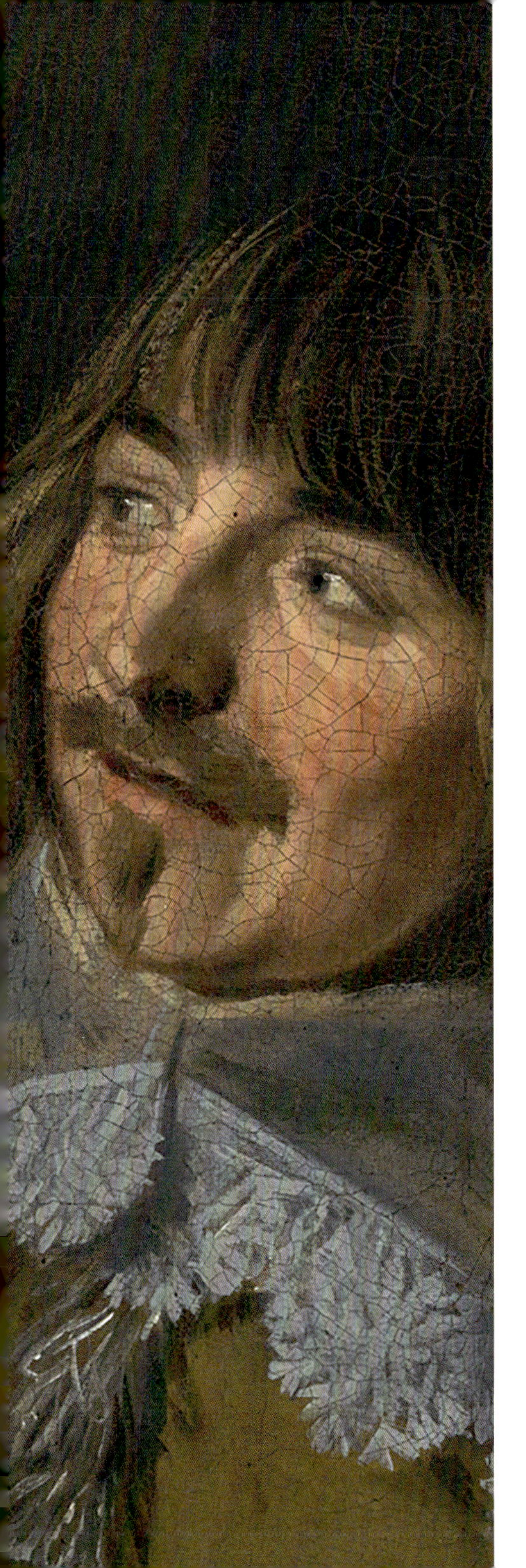

High lights Frans Hals Museum

Frans Hals Museum, Haarlem

Waanders Publishers, Zwolle

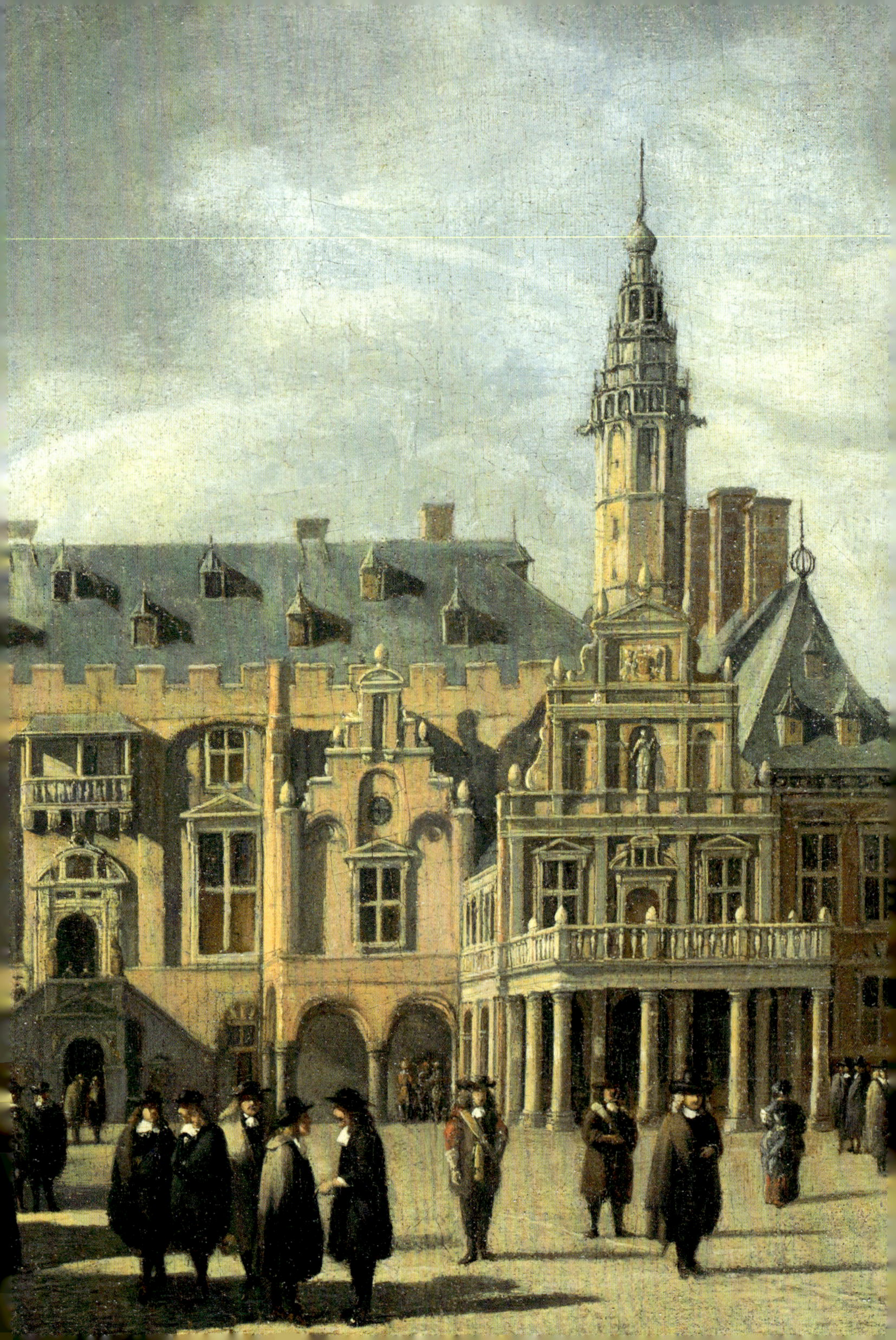

Highlights of the Frans Hals Museum

This book is intended as an introduction to the Frans Hals Museum and as a memento for visitors. Showcasing a selection of forty highlights, it demonstrates the richness and diversity of the collection. The museum is home to art of the past six centuries, from 16th- and 17th-century art to modern and contemporary art, from paintings to photography and video art, produced here in Haarlem or elsewhere, by internationally renowned artists.

A municipal collection

It all started with Haarlem town council, which in 1590 commissioned four paintings from Cornelis Cornelisz van Haarlem, one of the town's leading artists. The paintings were for the town hall on Grote Markt square, where the people of Haarlem and visitors could admire them.

Municipal Museum

Haarlem's art collection continued to grow over the years, with art taken over from disbanded institutions, including almshouses, orphanages and civic militias. This was how Frans Hals' civic guard portraits ended up in the collection. From 1862 onwards, visitors could admire the artworks in the Municipal Museum (or 'Stedelijk Museum'), housed in the town hall. Artists like Édouard Manet, Claude Monet, Max Liebermann and James McNeill Whistler came specially to Haarlem to see Frans Hals' paintings at the museum.

Groot Heiligland

Half a century later, the collection was moved from the town hall to the Oudemannenhuis, the former old men's almshouse, built in the early 17th century to accommodate poor men over the age of sixty. From 1810 the building on Groot Heiligland was used as an orphanage. In the early 20th century Haarlem municipal council had the former Oudemannenhuis converted into a new home for the Municipal Museum. It opened in 1913 under a new name, the Frans Hals Museum, after the most important artist in the history of the town. The name does not however mean that the museum's focus is exclusively on Hals' paintings – the forty highlights in this book show that there is much more to discover at the Frans Hals Museum.

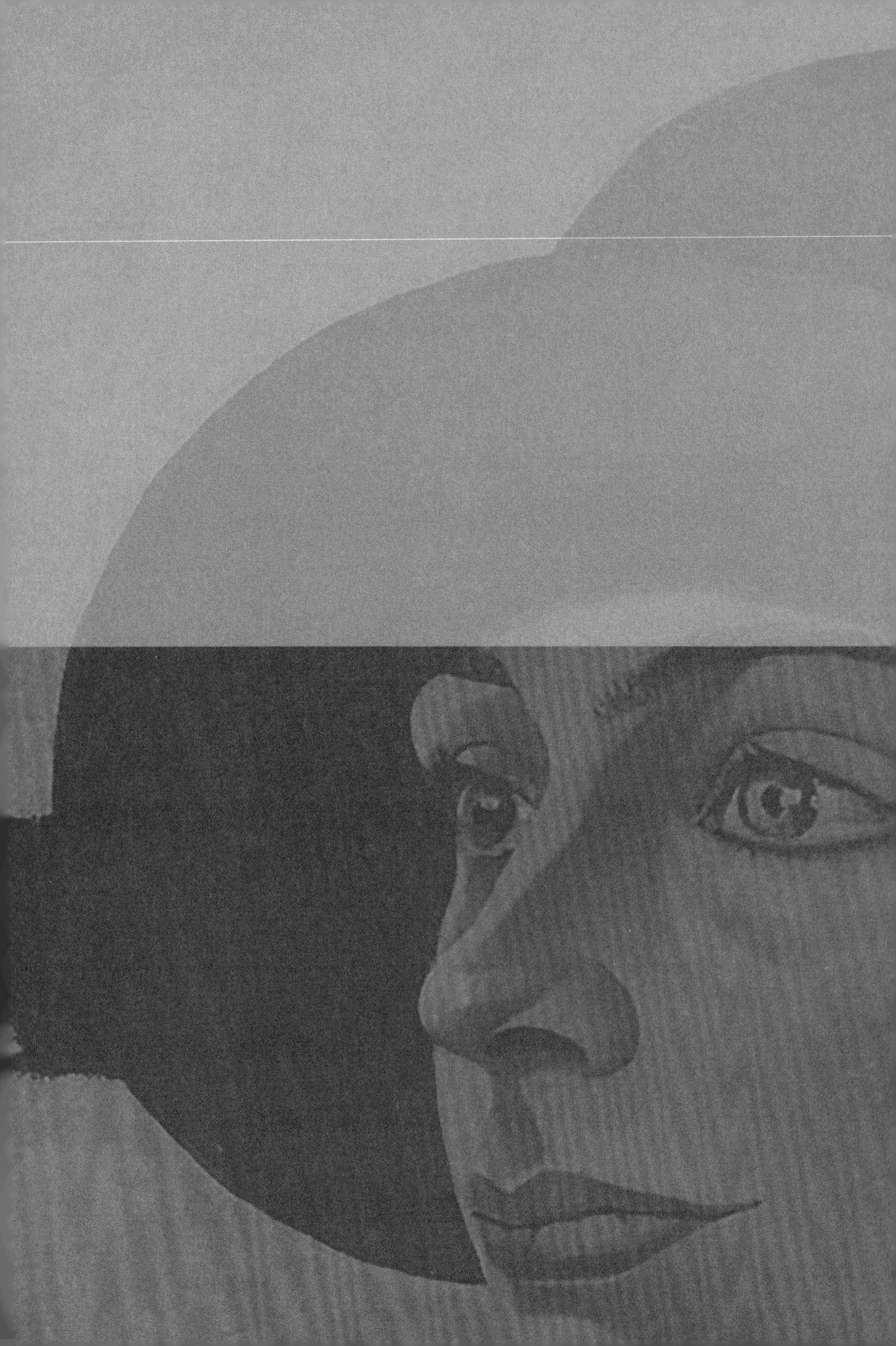

See Me

The Frans Hals Museum is home to many portraits. The oldest date from the 16th century, the most recent from the present day. They bring us face to face with people from a distant past or other parts of the world. Despite the fact that the portraits depict people from long ago and far away, they invite us to make eye contact, as if the subject were saying: see me, get to know me.

Love

Many of the portraits at the museum are by Frans Hals, who excelled at the lifelike depiction of his subjects. But there are also portraits by Hals' contemporaries, as well as by artists who came before and after him. Love of portraiture is as enduring as human love itself.

Why have your portrait painted? In the past people commissioned portraits to mark an important occasion, such as a wedding or a new appointment. People also had portraits made of their loved ones, so that they could keep them close. They also commissioned portraits to demonstrate their power and wealth. The civic guard portraits at the Frans Hals Museum are a good example of this.

Photography

Many people could not afford to have their portrait painted. That all changed in the 19th century, however, with the arrival of photography – a much less expensive technique. After a time, portraits were no longer the preserve of the elite, as people of lesser means were able to afford a photographic portrait. Now that almost everyone

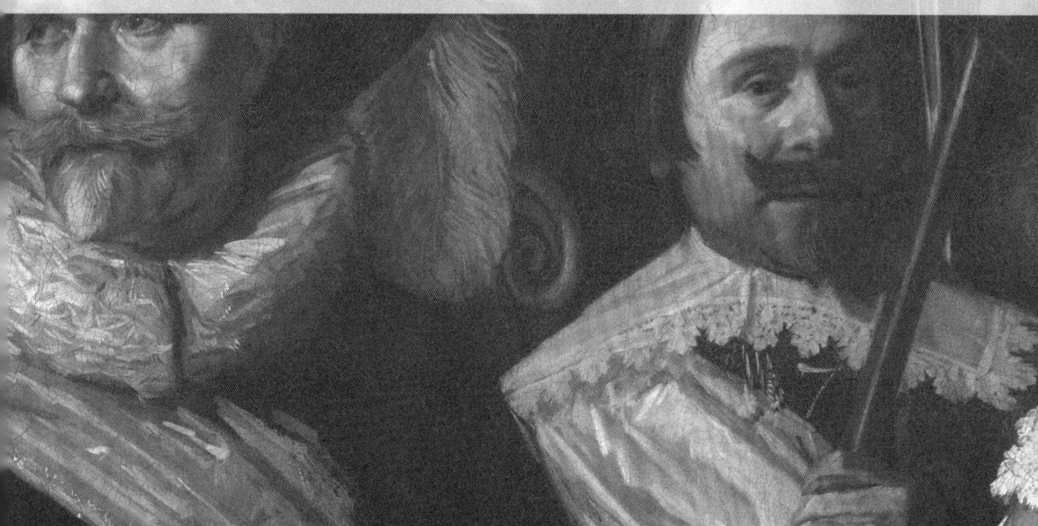

has a smartphone with a camera, there is no limit to the number of portraits we can create, of others and of ourselves.

Self-portraits

Artists not only produce portraits for others, they also make self-portraits. This gives them much more freedom to experiment, as they are not obliged to consider the wishes and expectations of their client. What's more, your own image in the mirror is always a cheap alternative, and a patient model.

Message

Artists – both those working in centuries past and more recently – often have an air of self-confidence in their self-portraits. Contemporary artists also use their own image to raise social issues. One example is the self-portrait by Sarah Lucas. This is more than simply a study of her image in the mirror. It also prompts us to reflect on the nature of femininity and masculinity.

Group portraits

Large group portraits are a Haarlem tradition that goes back centuries. The earliest examples were dignified and serious, but later they became distinctly more lively. Consider for example the large civic guard portraits by Frans Hals. But group portraits are not only a thing of the past, as exemplified by the piece which the museum commissioned from Iriée Zamblé. Her new group portrait puts Black women in the spotlight.

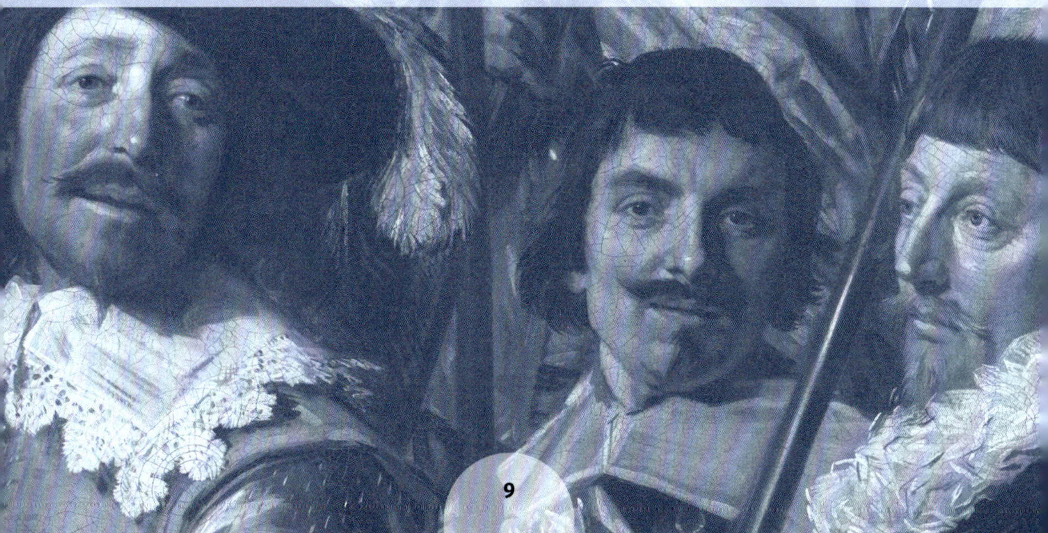

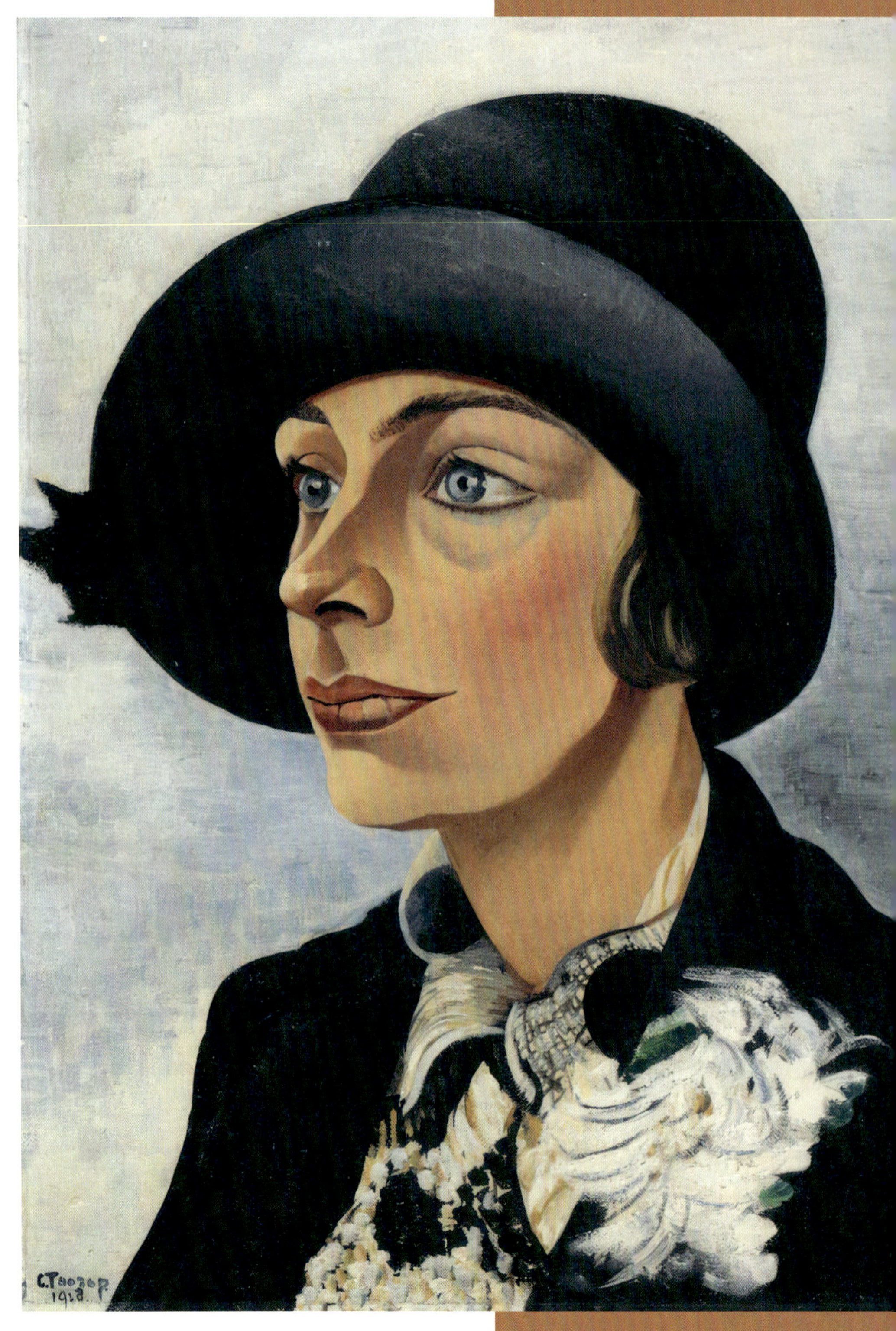
C.TOOROP
1928.

Charley Toorop

Katwijk, 1891 – Bergen, 1955

Woman in a Black Hat, probably Annie Oud-Dinaux, 1928

oil on canvas

Charley Toorop's portraits are known for their vivid colours, strong silhouettes and intense eyes, as in this portrait of a woman, probably Annie Oud-Dinaux (1893-1990). She was married to architect J.J.P. Oud, one of the leading lights of the De Stijl movement. Toorop painted the portrait when she was working with Oud on an exhibition at the Stedelijk Museum in Amsterdam. After Oud's death, Annie Oud-Dinaux preserved her husband's archive and legacy. It is partly thanks to her efforts that De Stijl is known around the world today.

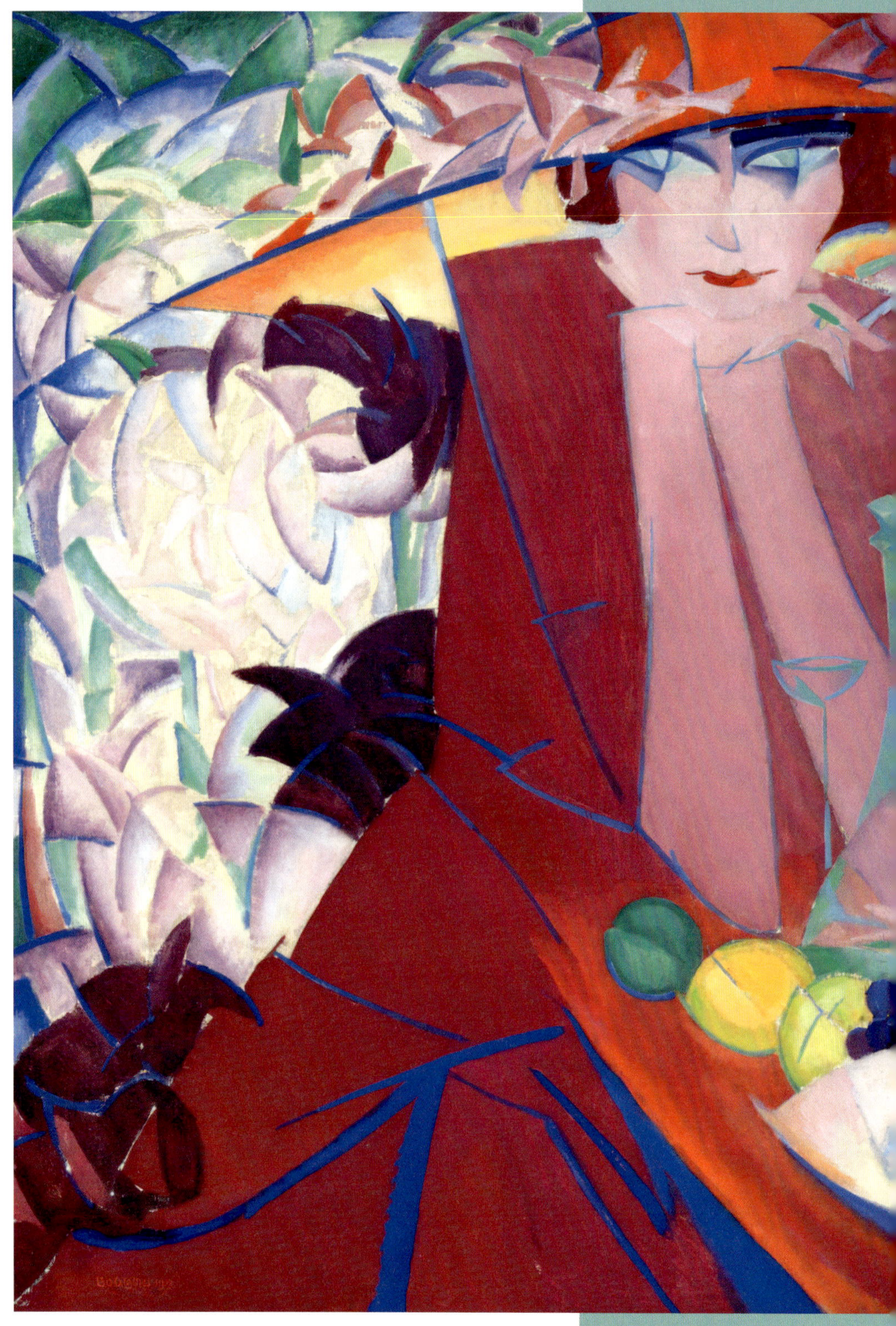

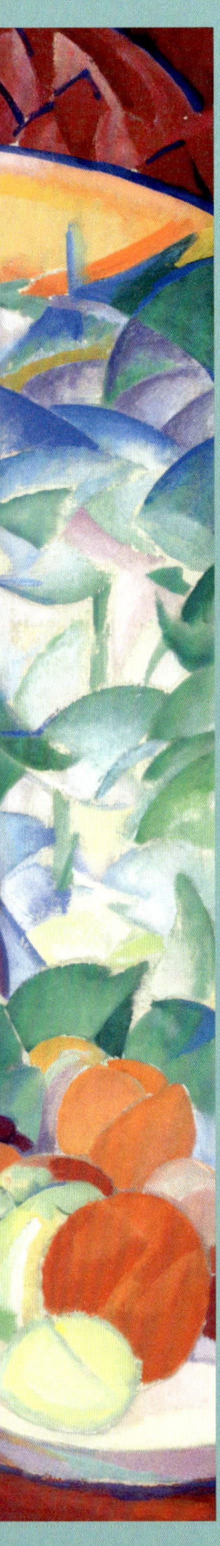

Leo Gestel

Woerden, 1881 – Hilversum, 1941

Woman in a Large Hat in a Summer House, 1913

oil on canvas

This is most likely Else Berg, a fellow artist and friend of Leo Gestel's. The two artists knew each other from Amsterdam and they worked together in Bergen, an artists' colony in the province of Noord-Holland. Berg is holding a cigarette, which was considered 'unfeminine' and thus controversial. Her boldness suited Gestel's experimental style perfectly – his brightly coloured painting is more an exercise in the latest angular style of the Cubist movement than a representative portrait.

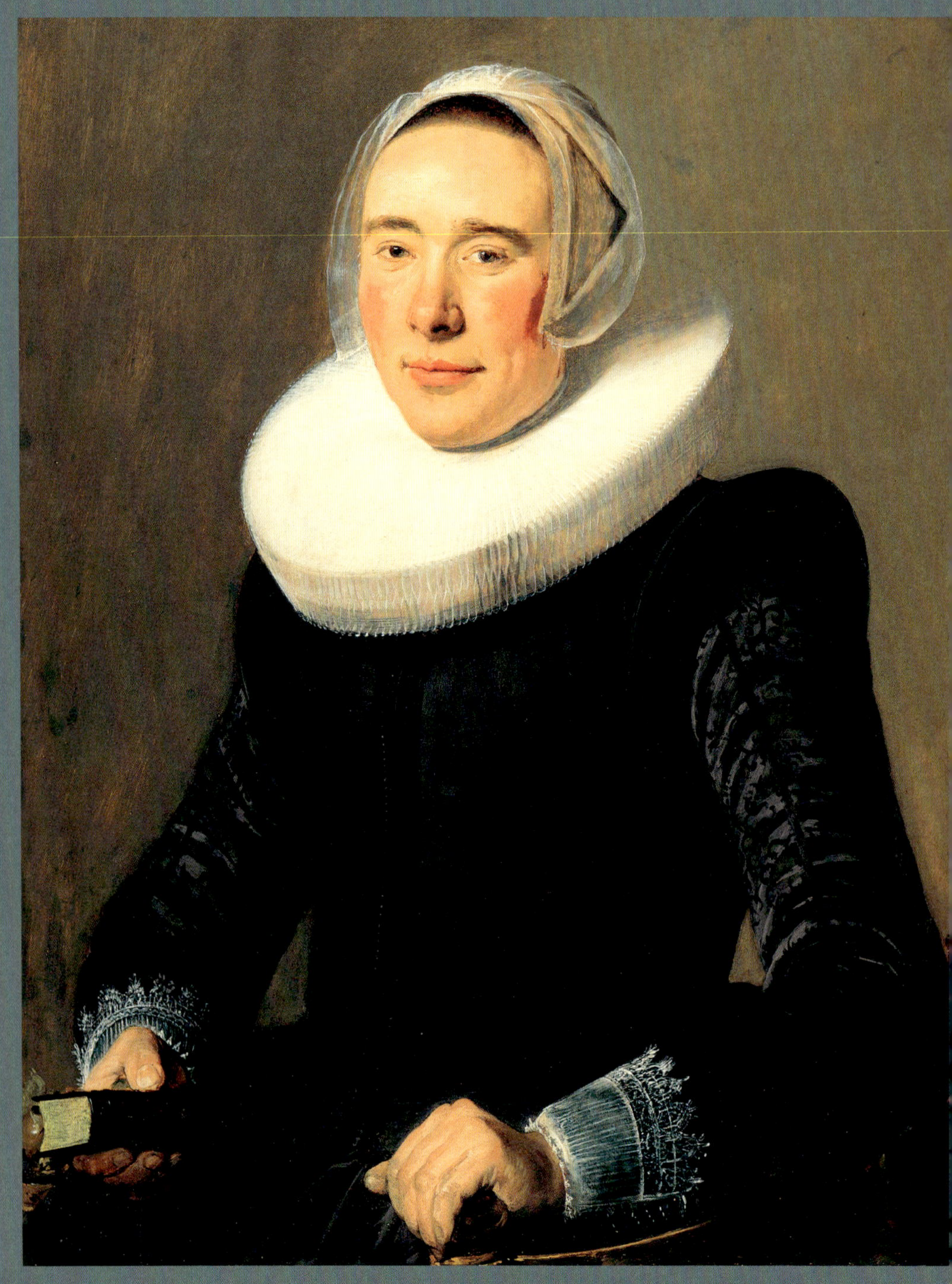

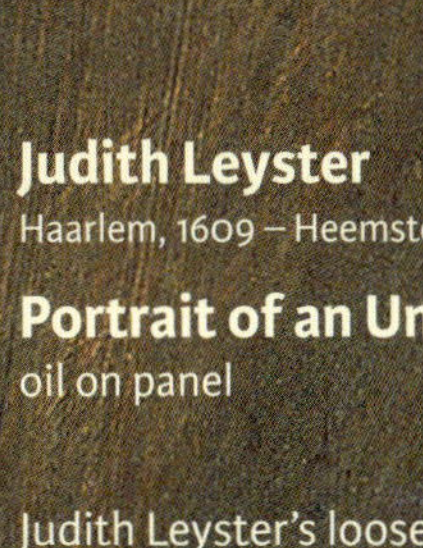

Judith Leyster

Haarlem, 1609 – Heemstede, 1660

Portrait of an Unknown Woman, 1635

oil on panel

Judith Leyster's loose brushwork is reminiscent of Frans Hals' style. As is this woman's cautious smile, which reveals a dimple in her cheek. This portrait was long thought to have been by Hals, until Judith Leyster's signature – *JL* with a star – was discovered.
In 1633 Leyster became a member of the Guild of St Luke, the professional association of painters. She was one of the first women in the Dutch Republic to become a member of a painters' guild.

acquired with the support of the Rembrandt Association

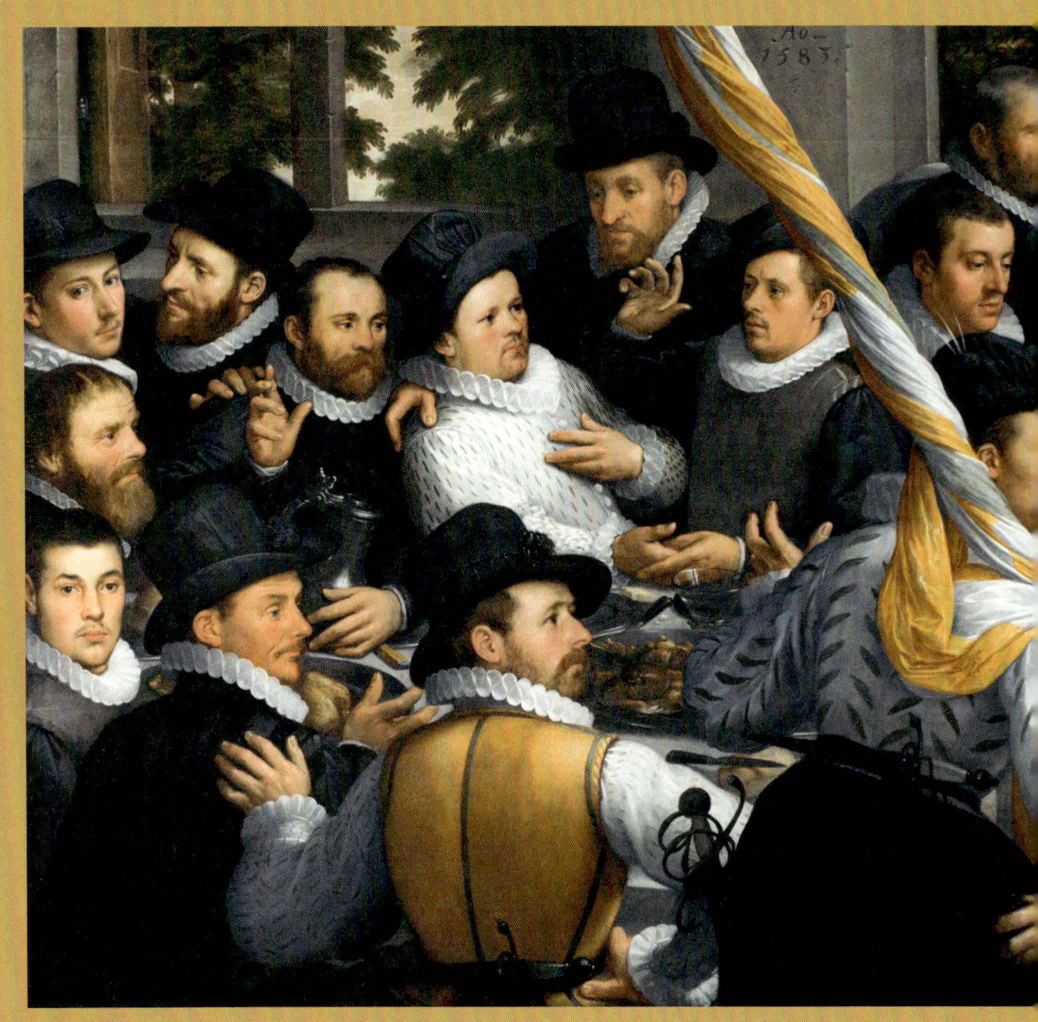
Ao
1583.

Cornelis Cornelisz van Haarlem

Haarlem, 1562 – Haarlem, 1638

Banquet of Members of the Haarlem Calivermen Civic Guard, 1583

oil on panel

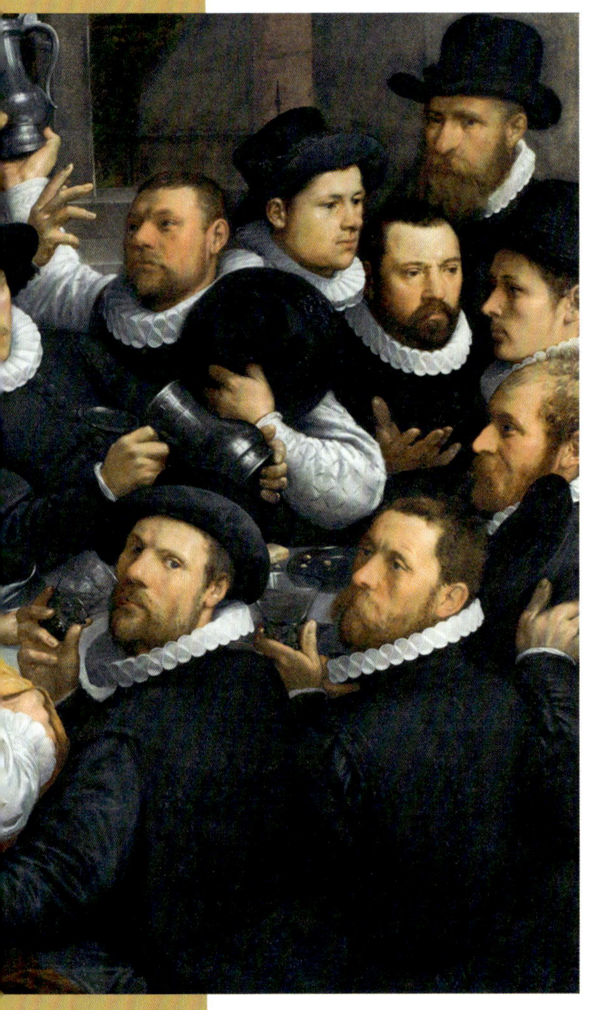

This festive banquet has turned into a lively event. The guardsmen are engaged in animated conversation, and are all in physical contact with each other. Cornelis van Haarlem portrayed the men in an innovative, spontaneous manner, a departure from the usual more formal group portraits. The furled banner that divides the composition diagonally was revolutionary too. Cornelis was actually part of this company. He is the man in the back left, looking directly at us, in what is Haarlem's earliest known civic guard portrait.

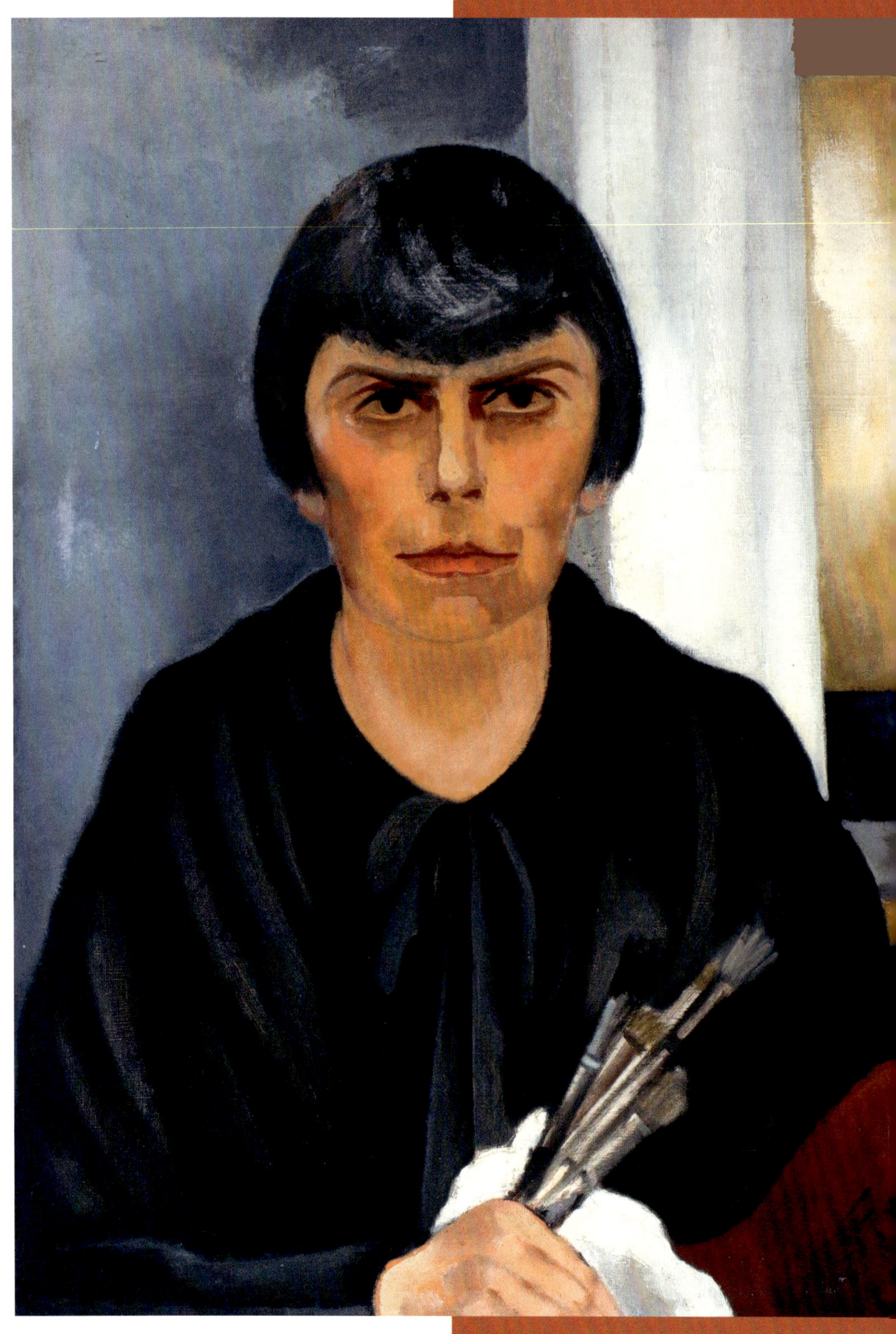

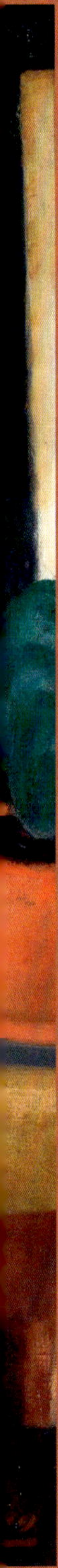

Else Berg

Ratibor (Poland), 1877 – Auschwitz (Poland), 1942

Self-Portrait with Brushes, *c.* 1929

oil on canvas

Else Berg's paintings brought her considerable success. This was unusual at a time when society offered few opportunities for women. She was in her fifties when she painted this self-portrait, presenting herself as a confident artist holding her brush and palette. Her piercing gaze recalls the work of Charley Toorop, and indeed Berg knew Toorop and her work well. The life and career of Else Berg, who was Jewish, came to an abrupt end when she was murdered by the Nazis in Auschwitz.

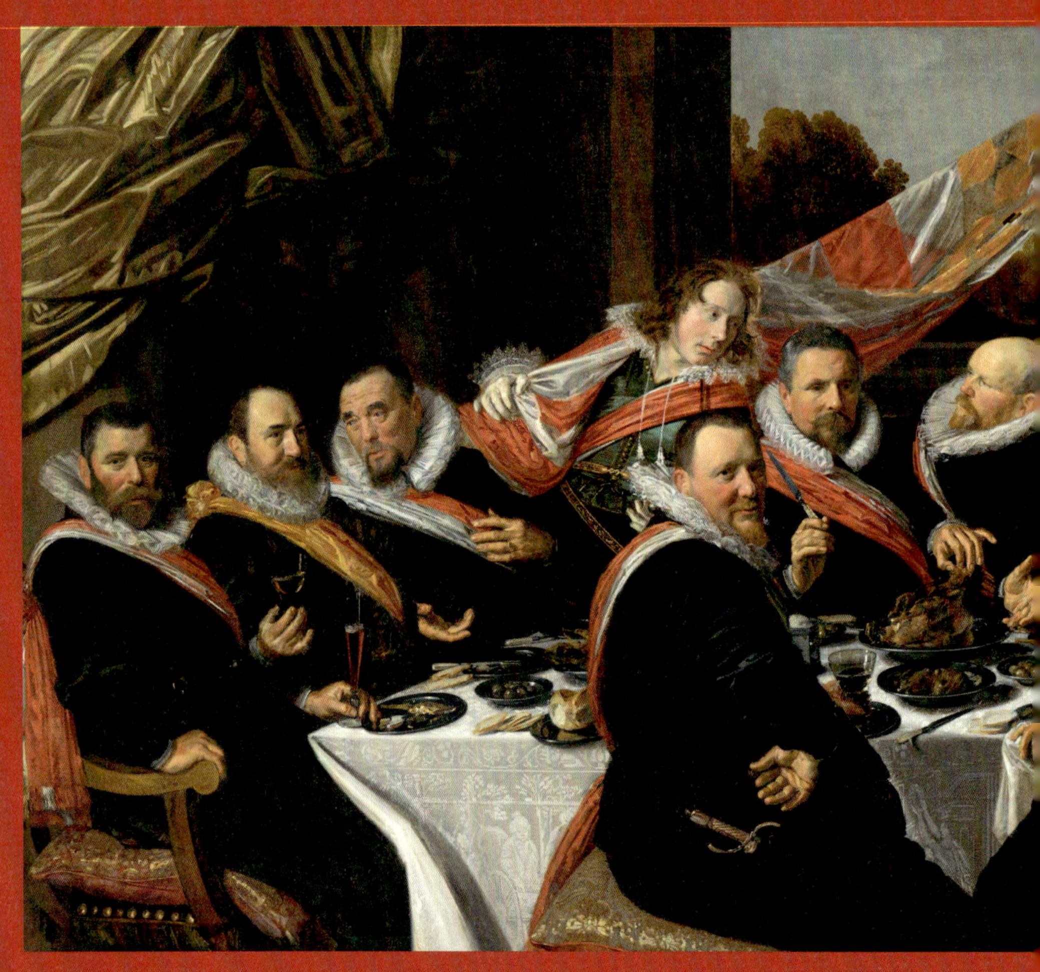

Frans Hals

Antwerp, *c.* 1583 – Haarlem, 1666

Banquet of the Officers of St George's Civic Guard, 1616

oil on canvas

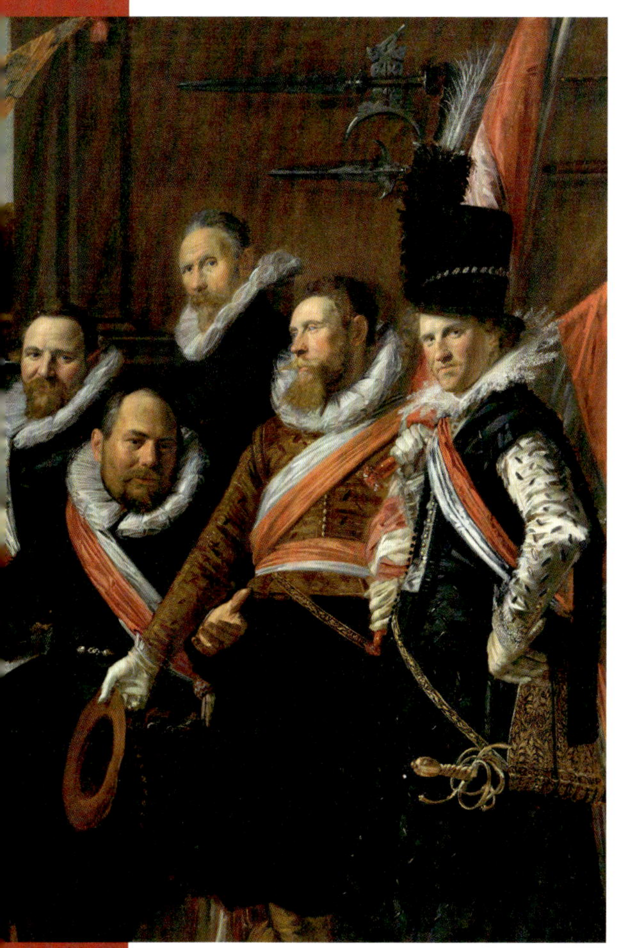

In the 17th century, civic militias, or civic guards, were a combination of police, fire brigade and army. Officers would hold banquets to celebrate their retirement from service, and often had the moment captured in the form of a group portrait.

This is Hals' earliest civic guard painting, and his very first large commission. His enormous talent was already apparent in this painting full of life and movement. The men chat to each other, and some look up at us, as if we had just entered the room.

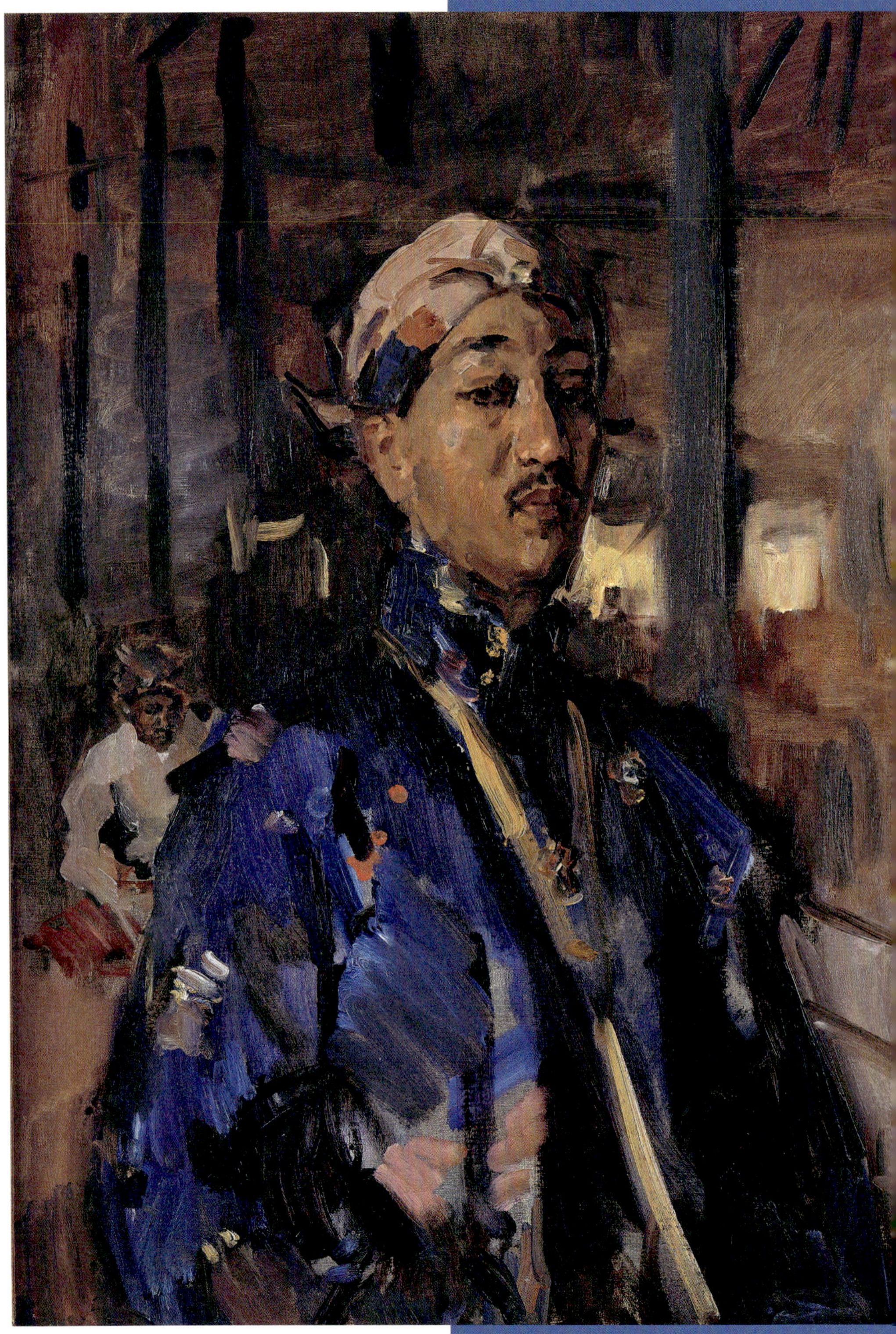

Isaac Israels

Amsterdam, 1865 – The Hague, 1934

Portrait of Mankunegara VII, a Javanese Ruler, 1922

oil on canvas

Mangkunegara VII was head of one of the four royal courts in Central Java from 1916 to 1944. At the time, Indonesia was a colony governed by the Dutch. Despite the unequal relationship, the Mangkunegara did have limited powers. He encouraged Javanese culture and science, in order to modernise his principality.

Isaac Israels painted this portrait with rapid brushwork, the broad strokes of pink and blue dancing on the canvas. This loose style was a bold and unusual step, as portraits of monarchs tended to be painted in much finer detail.

acquired with the support of the Rembrandt Association

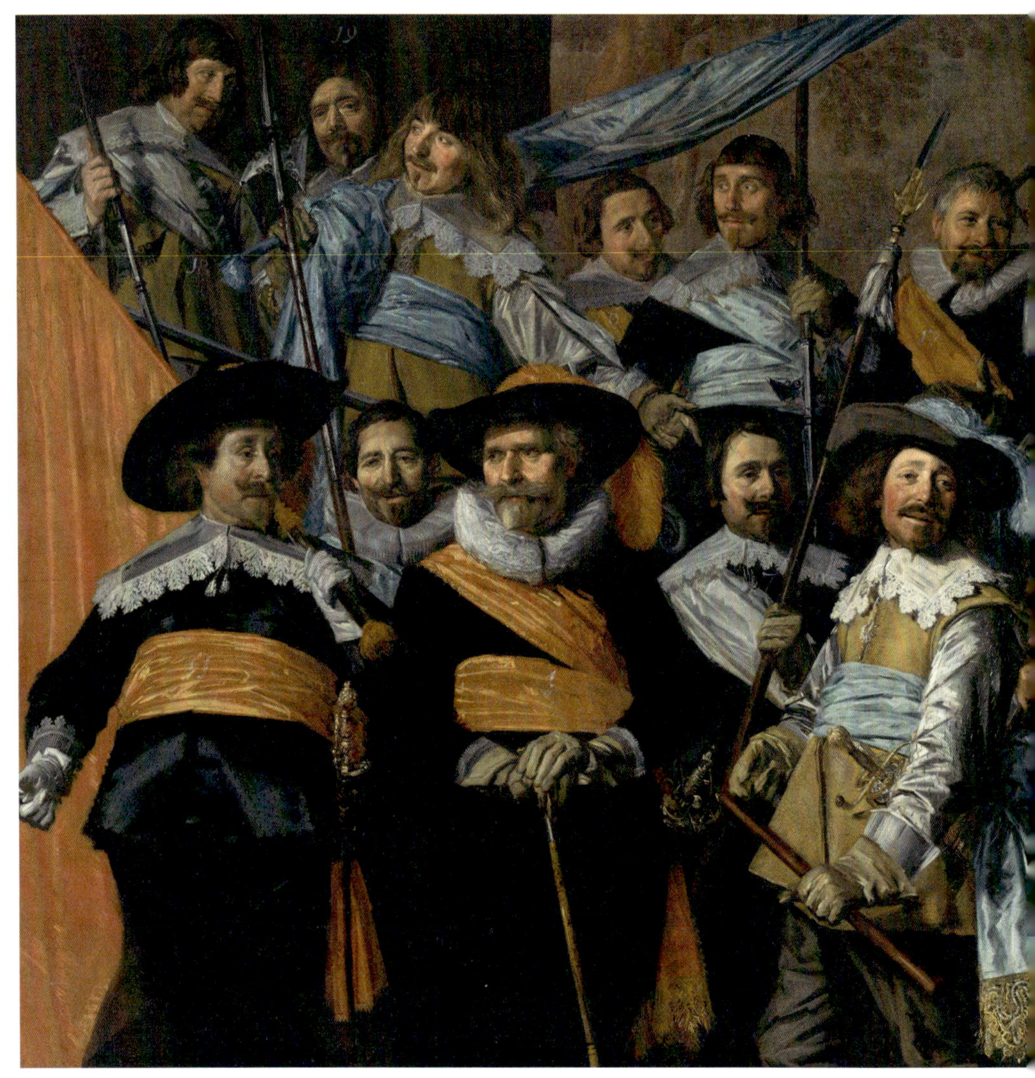

Frans Hals

Antwerp, *c.* 1583 – Haarlem, 1666

Officers and Sergeants of St George's Civic Guard, 1639

oil on canvas

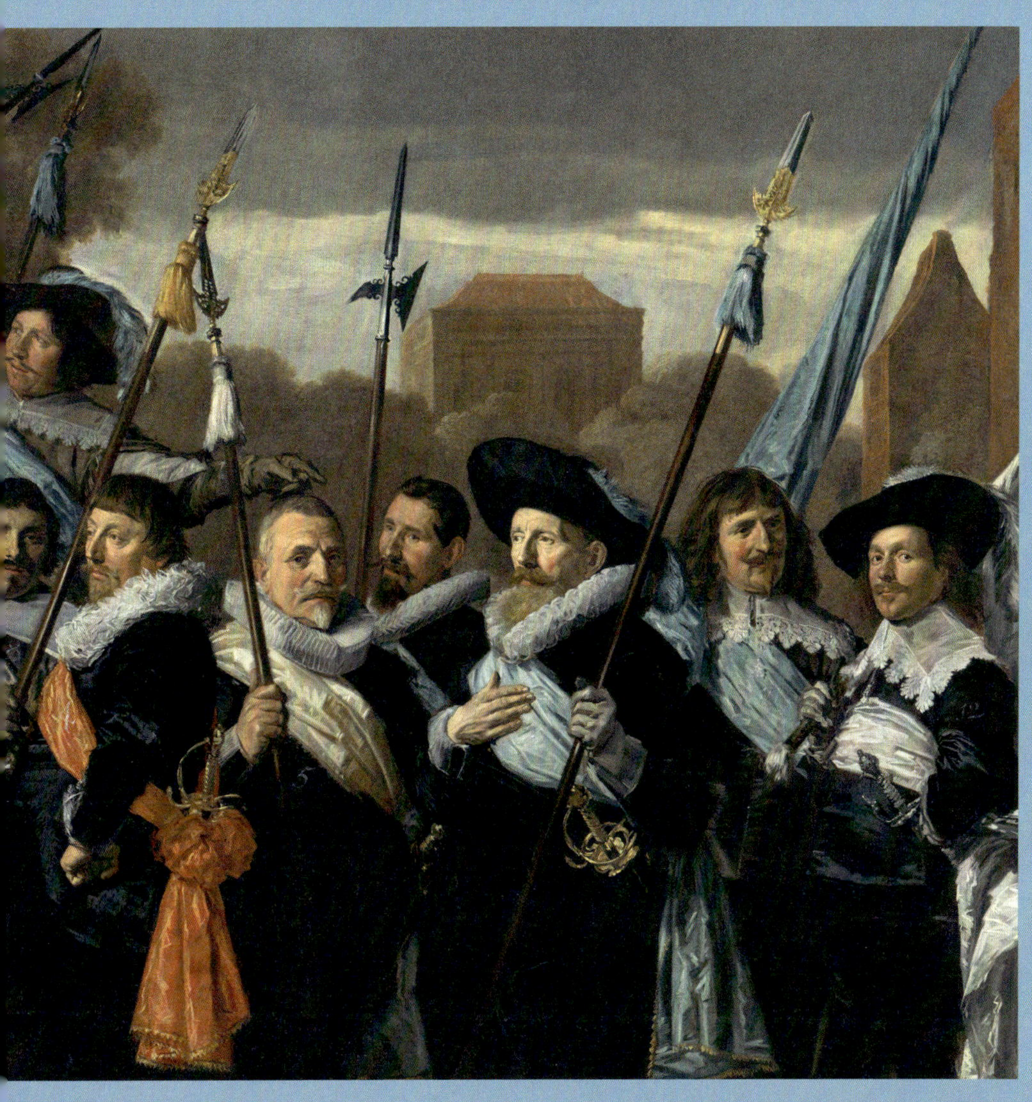

In 1639, the leaders of St George's civic guard commissioned Frans Hals to paint their group portrait again. It was his sixth and final civic guard painting. Here, the guards are not seated round a table, but are assembled in two rows – entirely unlike Hals' other group portraits. The sense of movement is created mainly by the weapons and banners.

Frans Hals included himself in the painting. The second man from the left in the back row is the only known self-portrait of Hals.

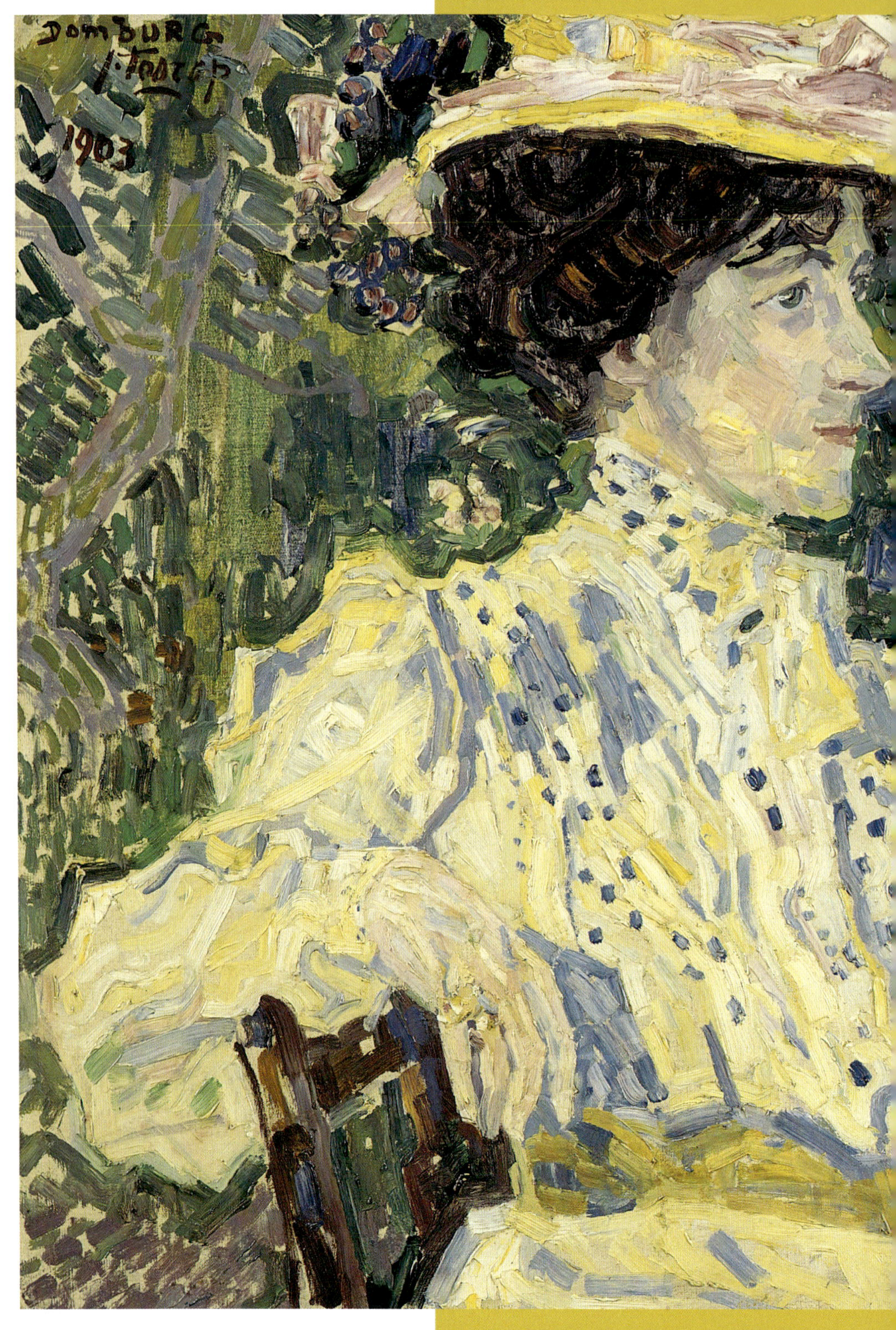
DomBURG
J. Toorop
1903

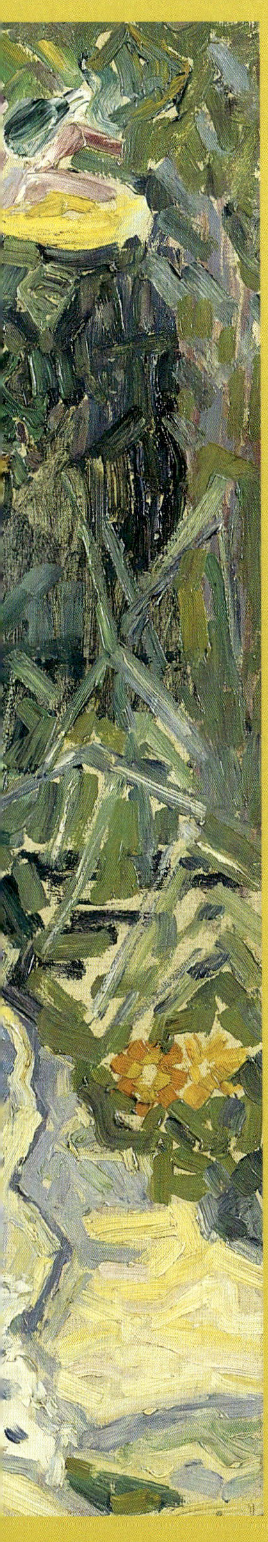

Jan Toorop

Purworejo (Indonesia), 1858 – The Hague, 1928

Portret van Elisa Beetz-Charpentier, 1903

oil on canvas

Jan Toorop gave this portrait the title *Madame B*, so it was long thought to be a portrait of his sister, Elize Beets-Toorop. But it is in fact Toorop's friend, the Belgian sculptor and jewellery maker Elisa Beetz (1859-1949). Beetz visited him in 1903 in the village of Domburg, where he painted her bathed in Zeeland's warm light. Two years later, she in turn portrayed Toorop in the form of a bronze mask.

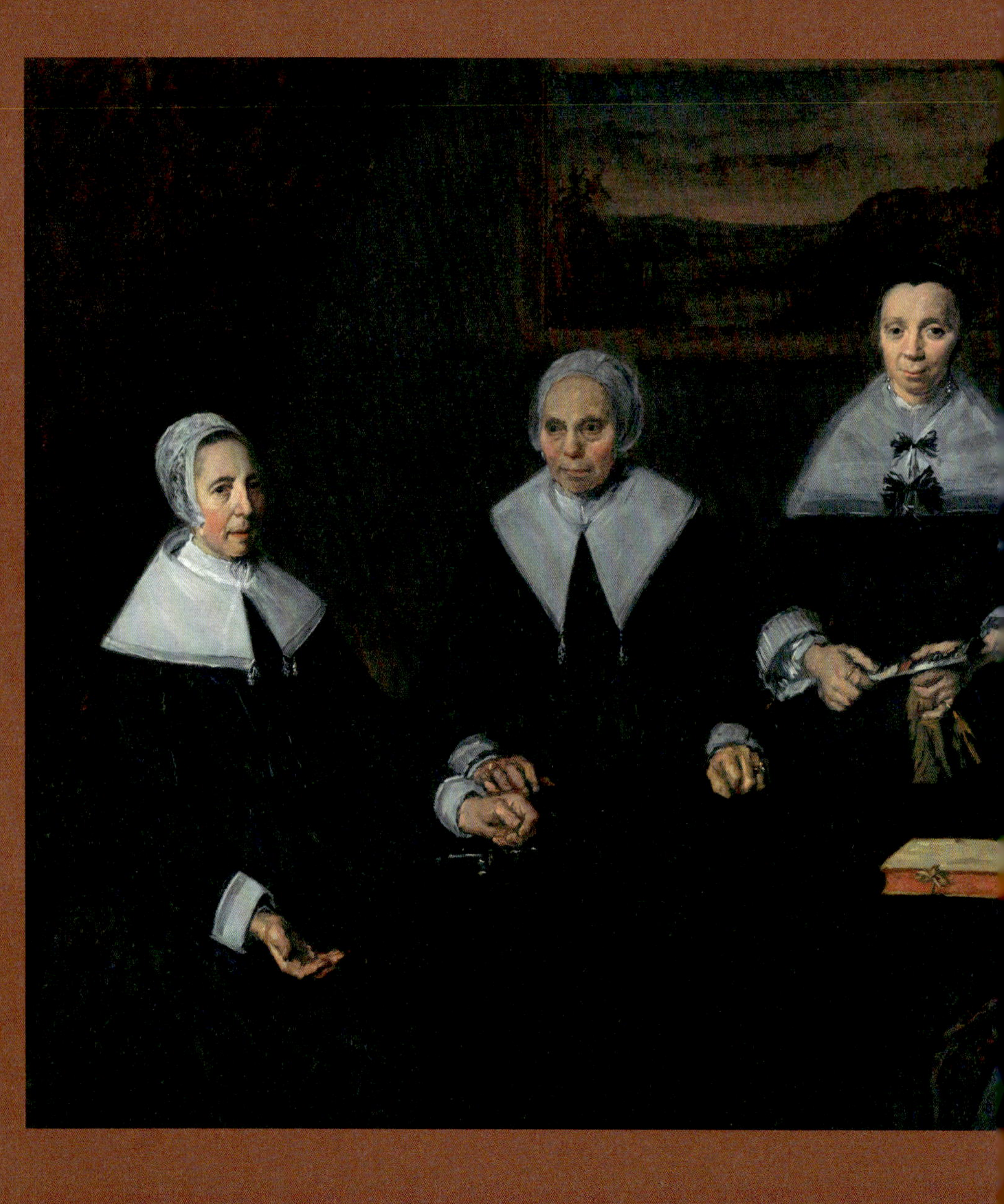

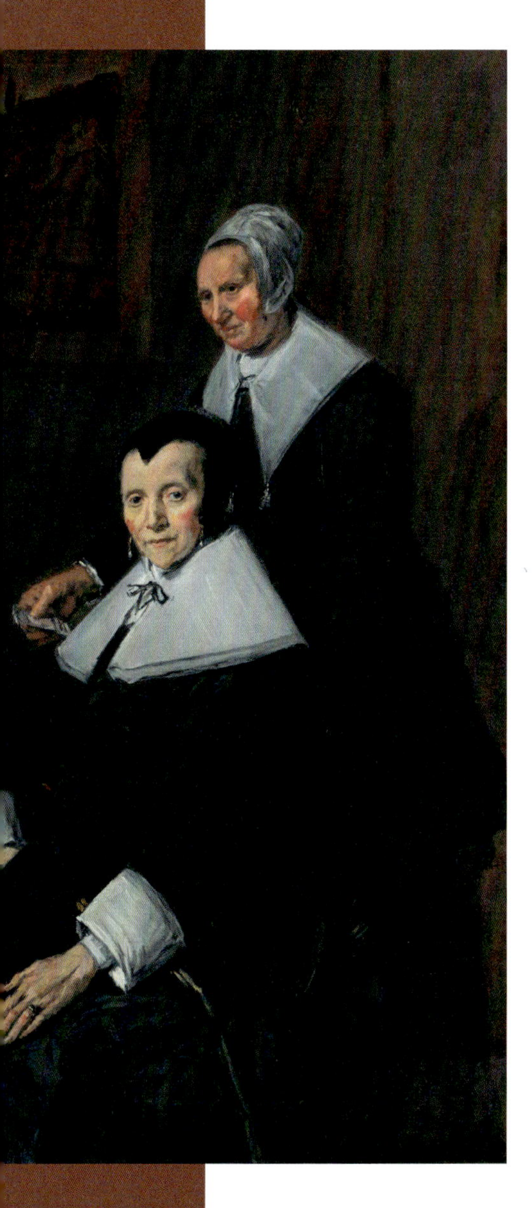

Frans Hals

Antwerp, *c.* 1583 – Haarlem, 1666

Regentesses of the Old Men's Almshouse, *c.* 1660

oil on canvas

Four women dressed in costly black gowns regard us from the canvas. They are the 'regentesses' – the female governors – of the Old Men's Almshouse ('Oudemannenhuis') in Haarlem. Standing behind them to the right is the 'house mother', who was responsible for the day-to-day running of the home, together with the 'house father'. Frans Hals was an old man himself – well into his seventies – when he portrayed the regentesses. He painted them very loosely, using coarse, wide brushstrokes – his signature style.

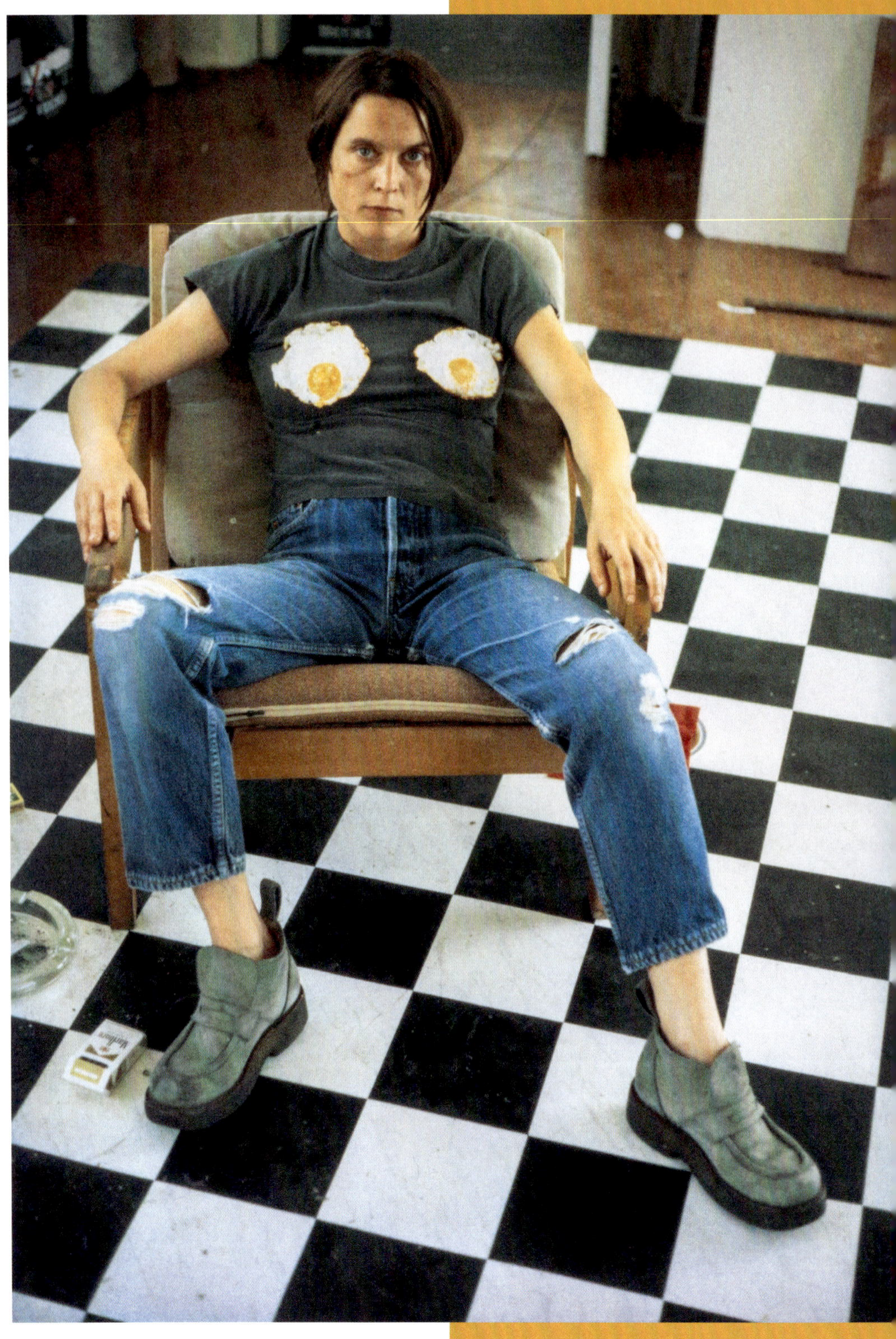

Sarah Lucas

b. 1962, London

Self-Portrait with Fried Eggs, 1996

photograph on watercolour paper

This is a self-portrait of British artist Sarah Lucas. Her attitude is butch and her expression serious, but the fried eggs on her chest introduce a lighthearted note of humour. Lucas plays with assumptions about gender, combining her 'masculine' appearance with the fried eggs, a reference to the female body. She sets out to make the viewer aware of the ideas that affect the way we look at each other. "I tried to imagine a world where women were seen in the same way as men."

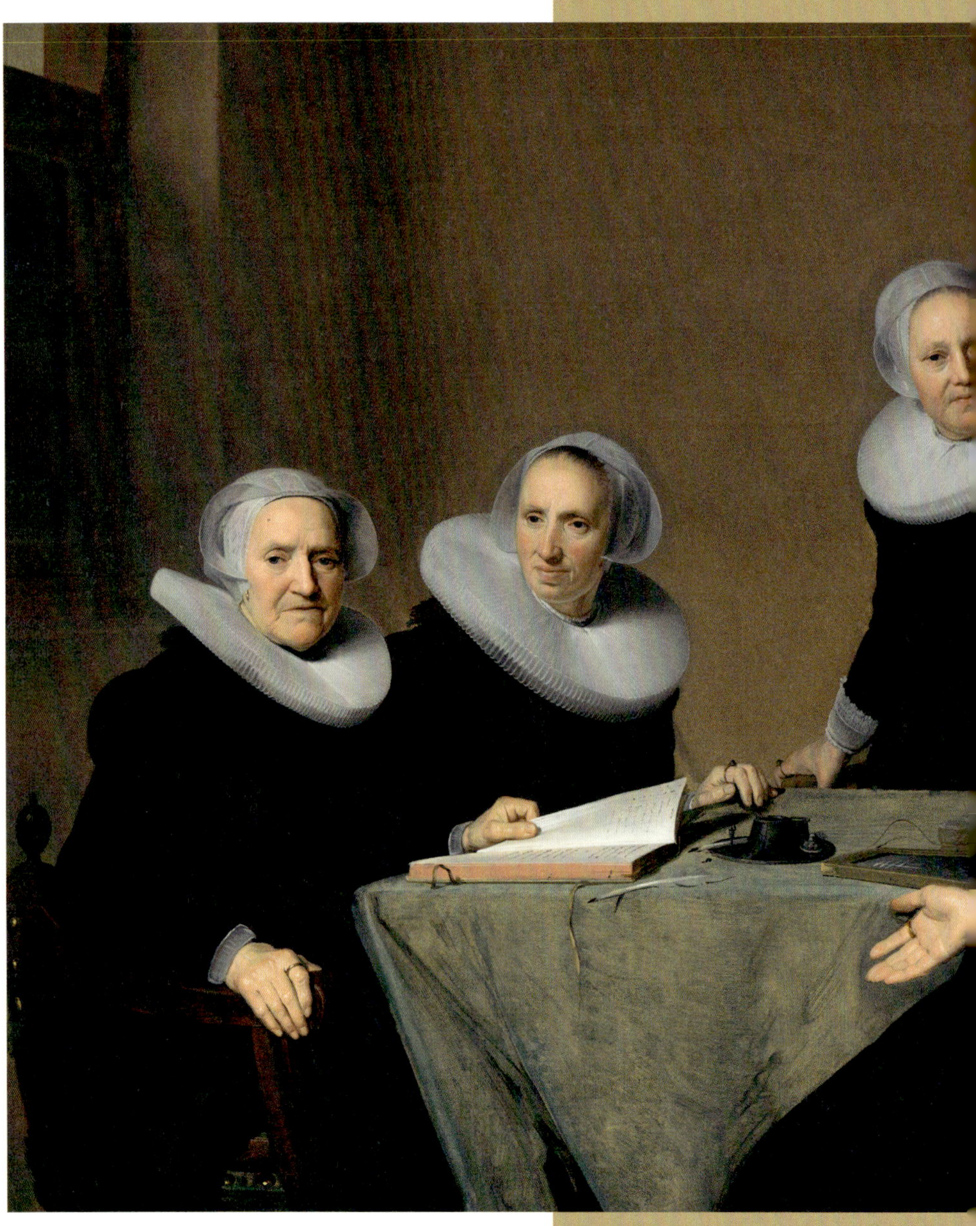

Johannes Cornelisz Verspronck

Haarlem, 1601/03 – Haarlem, 1662

Regentesses of St Elisabeth's Hospital, 1641

oil on canvas

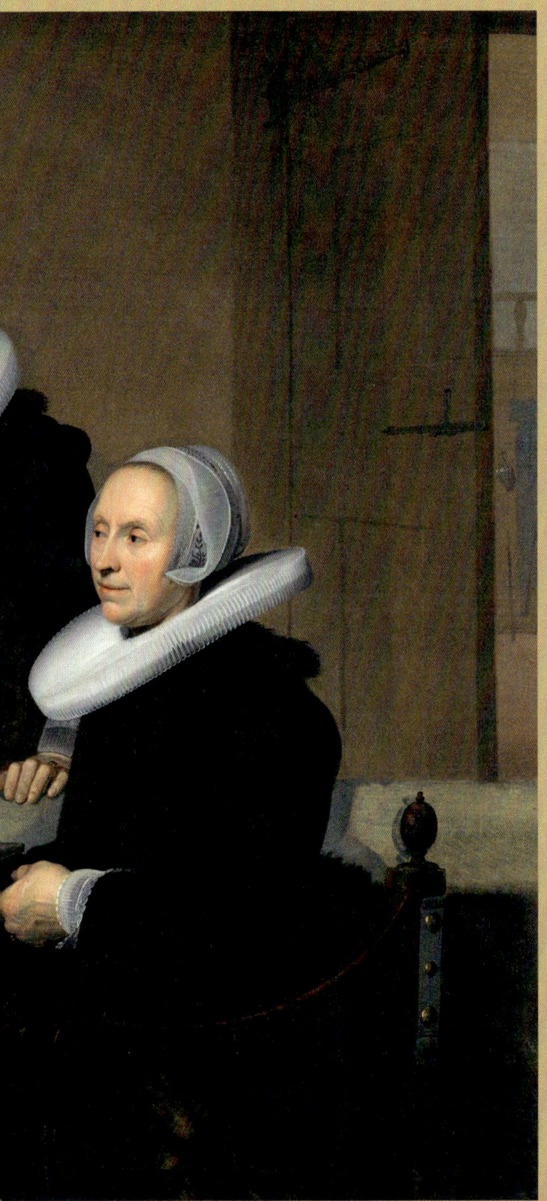

Saint Elisabeth's Hospital was a Haarlem charity run by governors ('regents' and 'regentesses'). In 1641 the regentesses on the board at the time commissioned Johannes Verspronck to paint their portrait. This was Verspronck's first major group portrait. He had a smooth and refined style, a great contrast with the loose brushwork of Frans Hals. Verspronck painted the women seated at a table, engaged in serious business as they look up at the artist – or maybe at us.

gift of the Elisabeth van Thüringen Fund

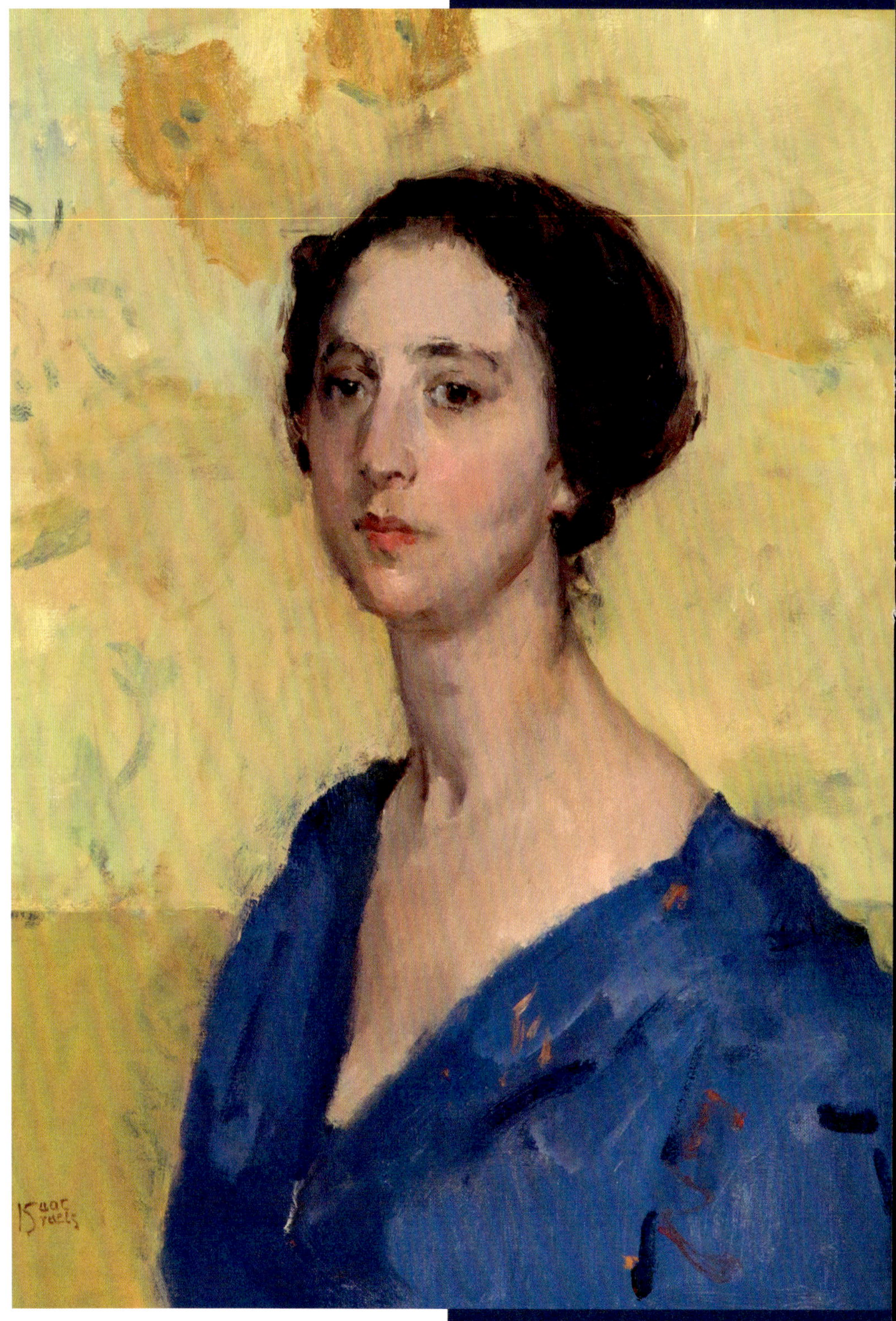

Isaac Israels

Amsterdam, 1865 – Den Haag, 1934

Portrait of Rosalie Zélander-Caffé, 1917

oil on canvas

Isaac Israels borrowed Vincent van Gogh's *Sunflowers* (1889) for a time, and used it in several portraits, including this image of Rosalie Zélander-Caffé. Israels admired Van Gogh's use of colour, as reflected in the contrast between the deep blue of her clothes and the yellow flowers.

Zélander-Caffé, who was Jewish, survived the Shoah, the persecution of Jews during the Second World War. She left this portrait and ten other modern artworks to the Frans Hals Museum.

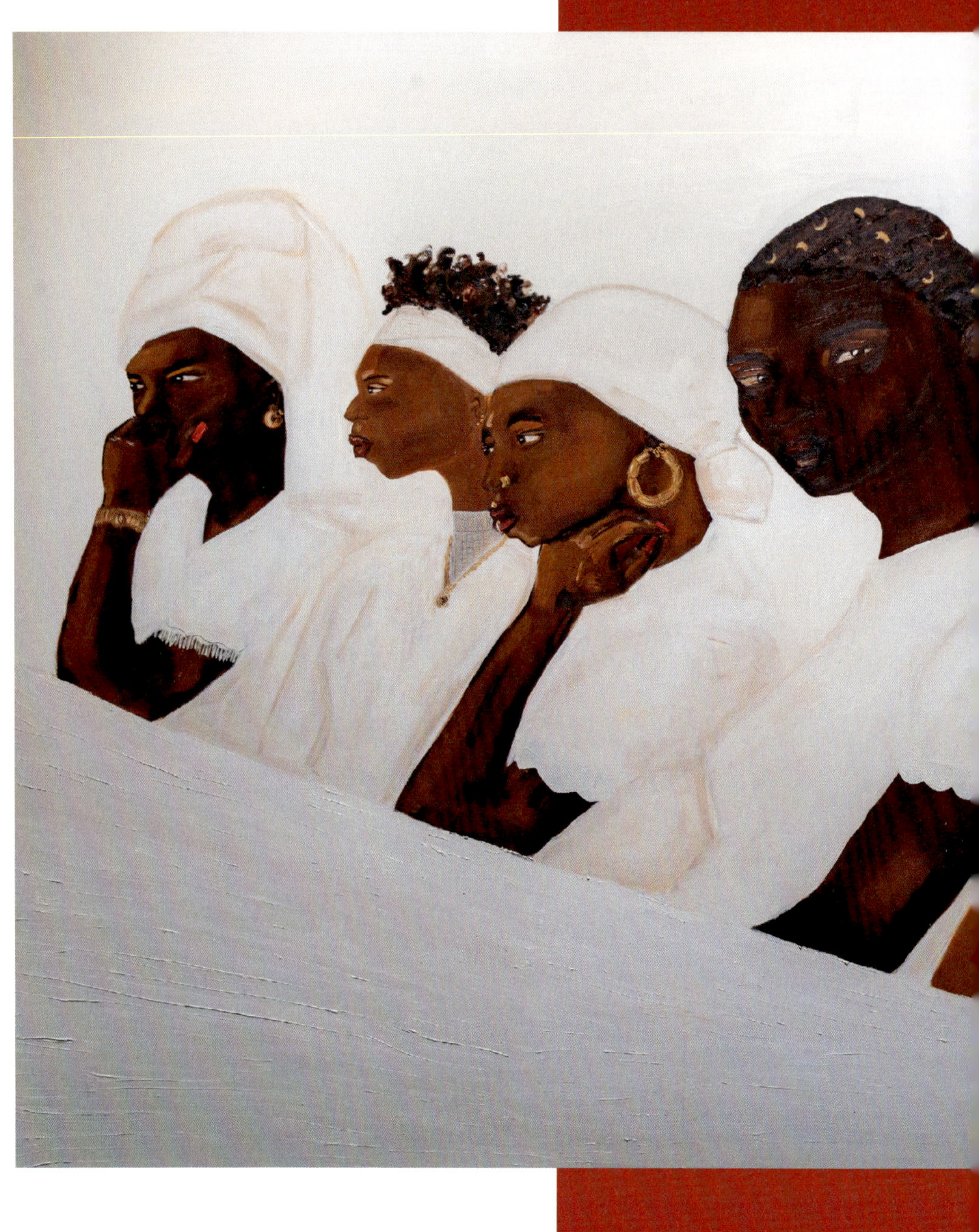

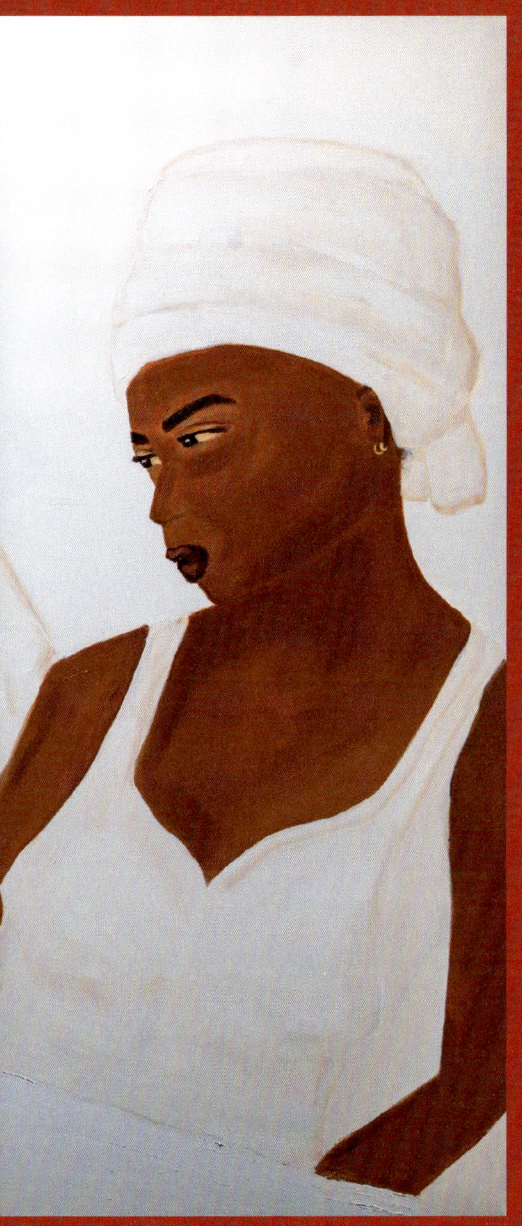

Iriée Zamblé

b. 1995, Amsterdam

Wishing on a Star, 2024

oil on canvas

Iriée Zamblé depicts fictional people who emerge during the painting process, as she explores the conventions of portraiture. Her work is inspired by research into Black identity and by West African and Dutch heritage: "I discovered how the slave trade contributed to making Haarlem rich and powerful in the 17th century. People were traded in exchange for Haarlem's cloth. So the 'dazzling white fabric' from Haarlem became the inspiration for this painting."

commissioned by the Frans Hals Museum and acquired with the support of the Friends of the Frans Hals Museum and the Mondriaan Fund

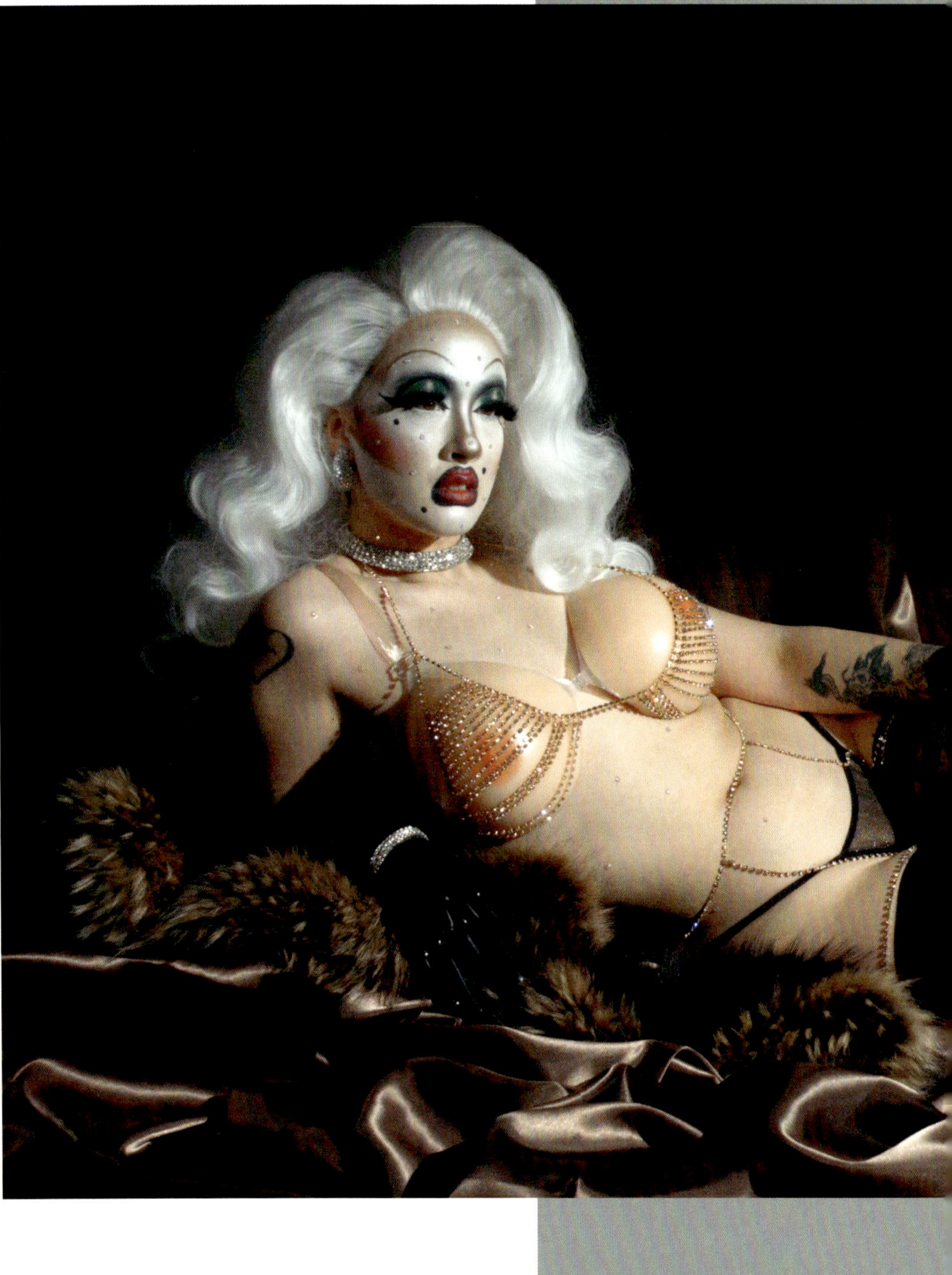

Sin Wai Kin

b. 1991, Toronto

Act I Part I, Tell me everything you saw, and what you think it means, 2018

video, 5:38 min

Make-up and costumes play an important role in the work of Sin Wai Kin, and are a way to bring their imagination to life. Sin creates characters who embody ideas about culture and identity. They are inspired by art history and pop culture, including the female nude and the stereotypical Hollywood ideal of beauty. In this video work Sin uses a 'hyperfeminine' drag character with a platinum blonde wig, silicon breasts and high heels. They prompt us to consider a possible future – also known as 'speculative fiction' – in which we are not constrained by binary notions of gender and beauty.

acquired with the support of the Mondriaan Fund and the Friends of the Frans Hals Museum

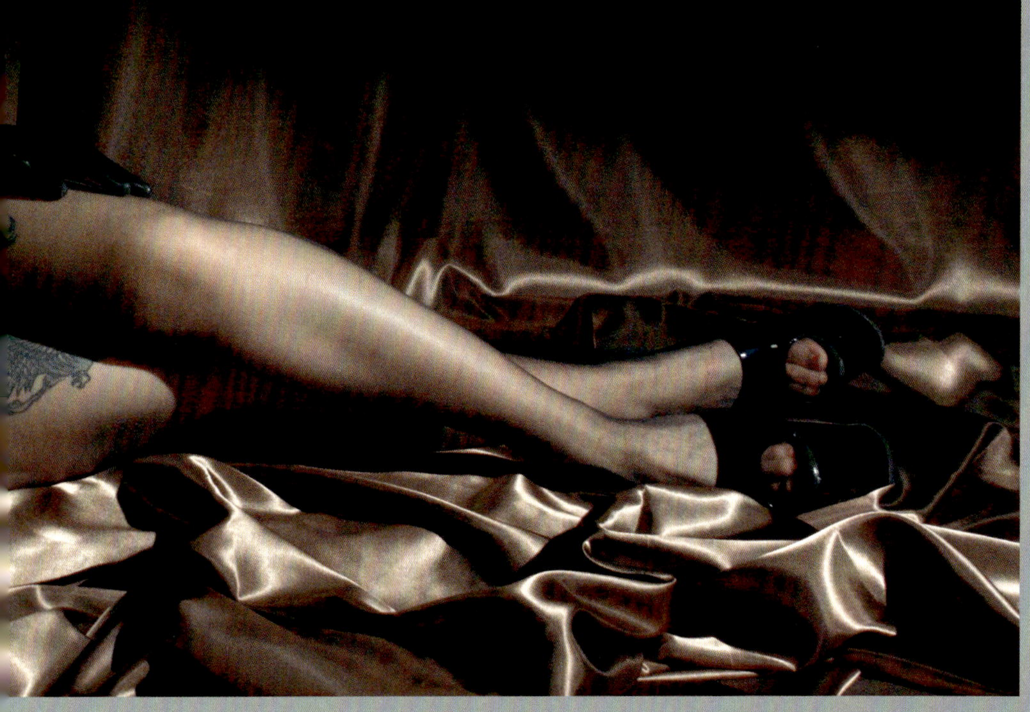

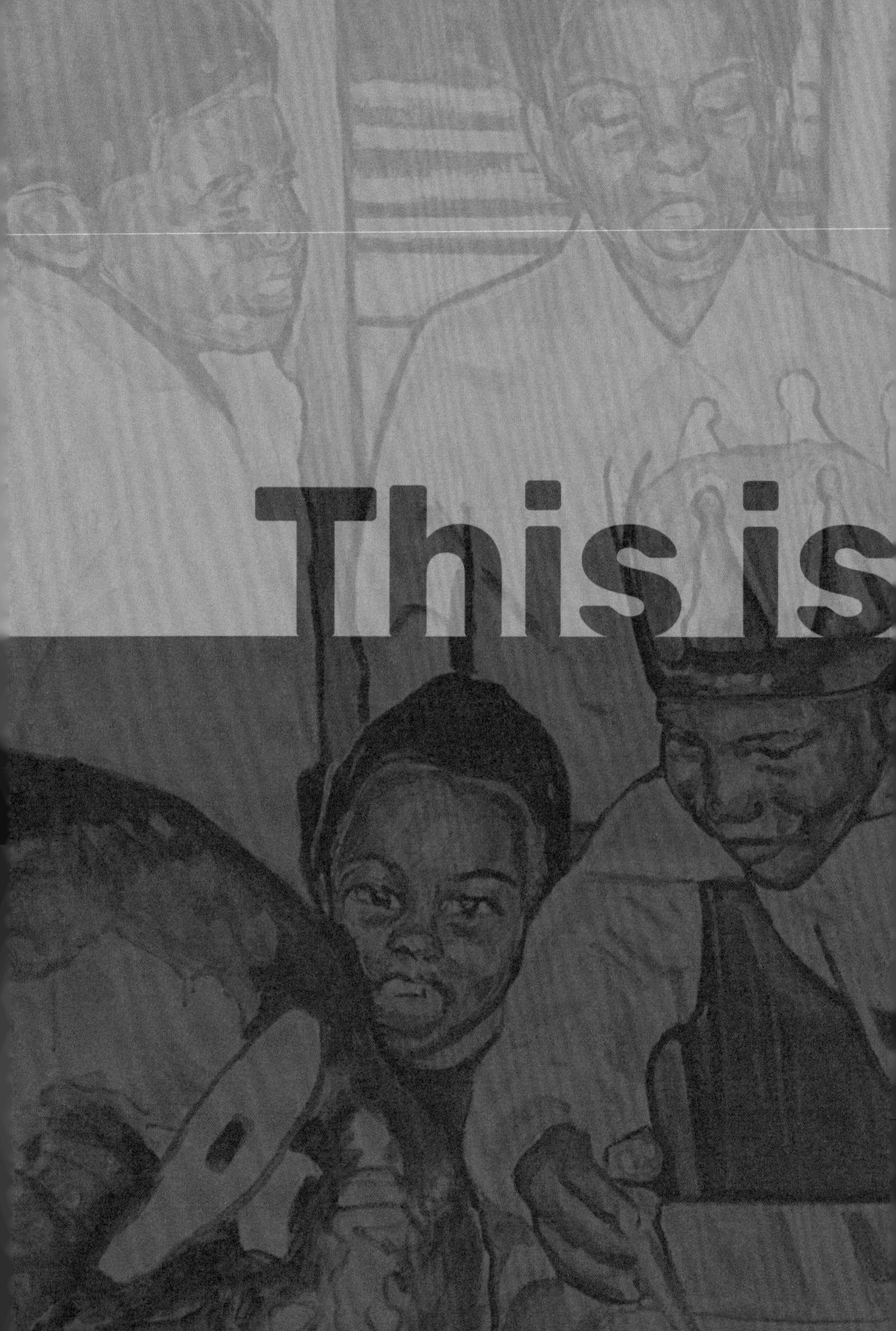
This is

Home

In the 17th century artists tended to depict their own surroundings – townscapes and landscapes, for example. This catered to the preferences of a new group of customers – wealthy merchants and governors – who felt more at home with the world they could see around them than with religious images that had a deeper meaning. We get a glimpse inside the homes of wealthy Dutch people in the 18th century in their doll's houses – miniature versions of the ideal home.

Still lifes

Art lovers in the 17th century also liked to hang still lifes in their homes, images of subjects they knew or used at home. These included tables laden with objects and foodstuffs from near and far, like a partially eaten pie, a pouch of tobacco or fine table linen. The most important thing in these images is the rendering of the different materials, preferably as naturalistic as possible, and with realistic light effects. Light reflects differently off a silver beaker than a pewter plate, linen napkin or juicy lemon, for example.

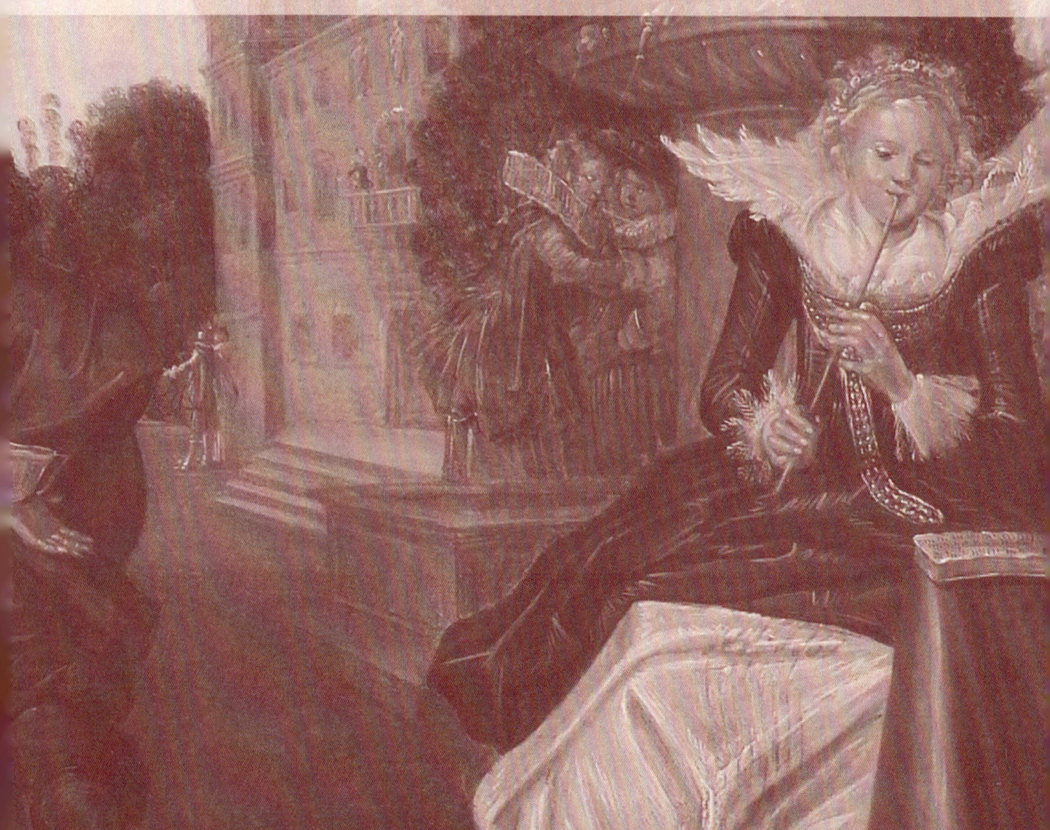

Food

Home is where you can be yourself and live by your own rules – alone, with loved ones, with friends. For many people, home is also associated with food, which can help us feel a connection with others, even if they live on the other side of the world, or are no longer with us. Food says something about you, defines your identity. To Benjamin Li, food is even a way of exploring his family history.

Going out to come home

Your identity is determined not only by what you eat and how you spend your day. For many people, in fact, nighttime is when they can truly be themselves. At a club or bar, you can finally abandon the rules and expectations of the day, partying together, dancing, free of everyday concerns. When you truly feel free to be yourself, going out is like coming home.

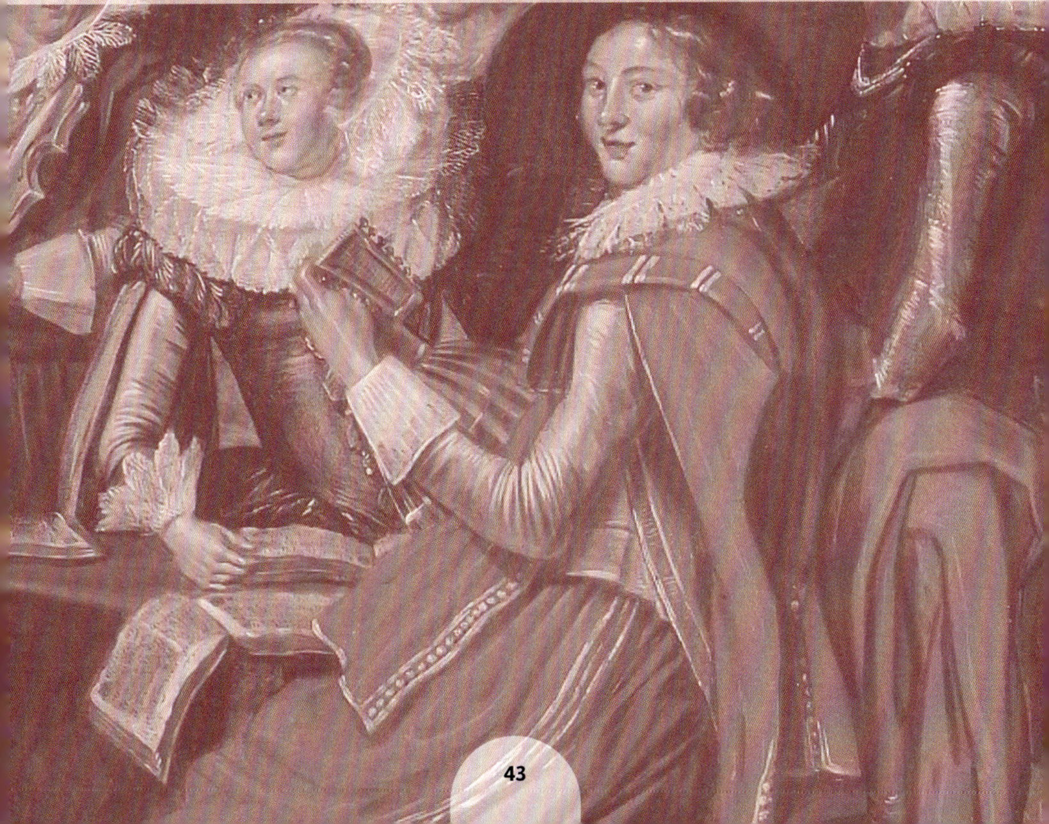

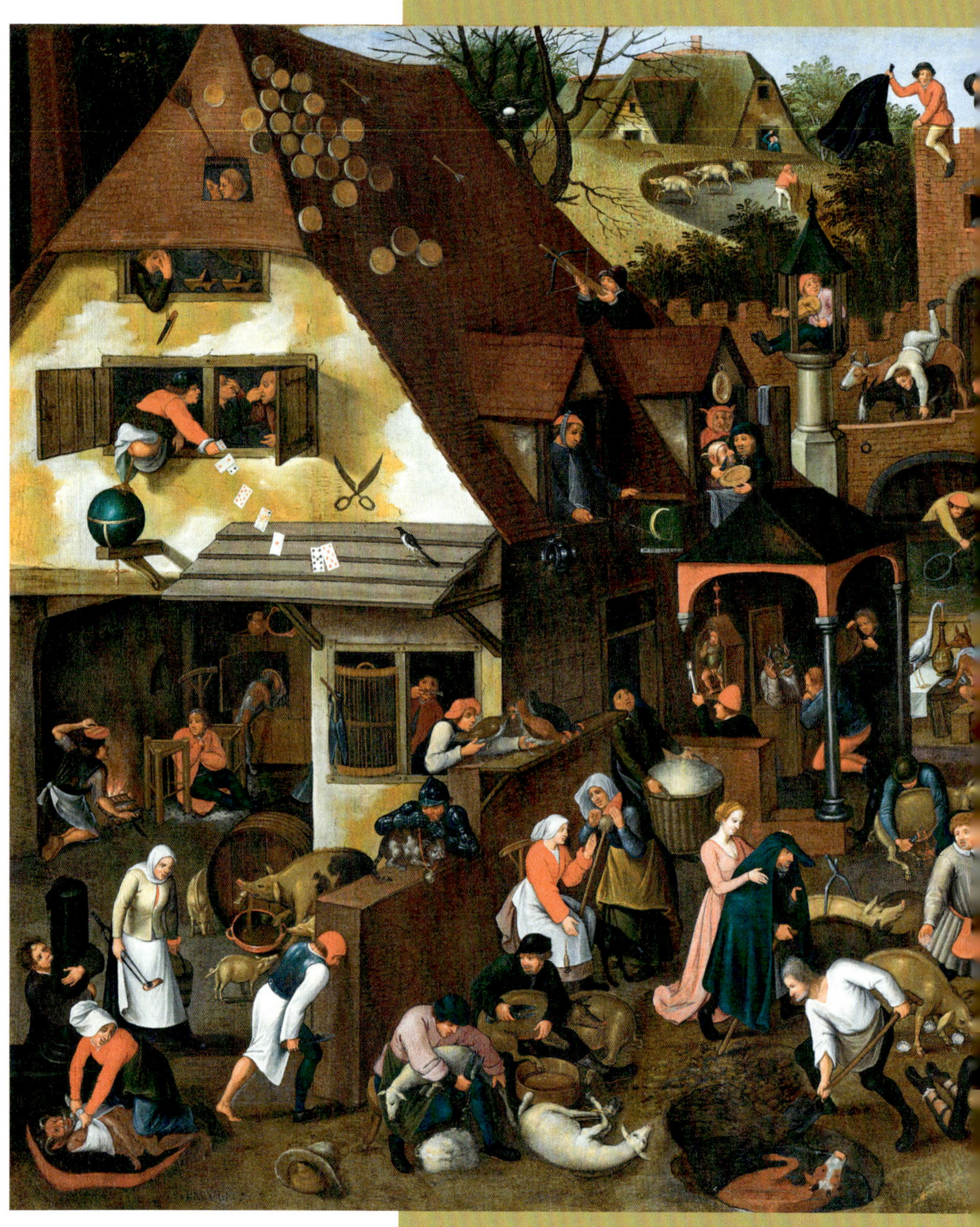

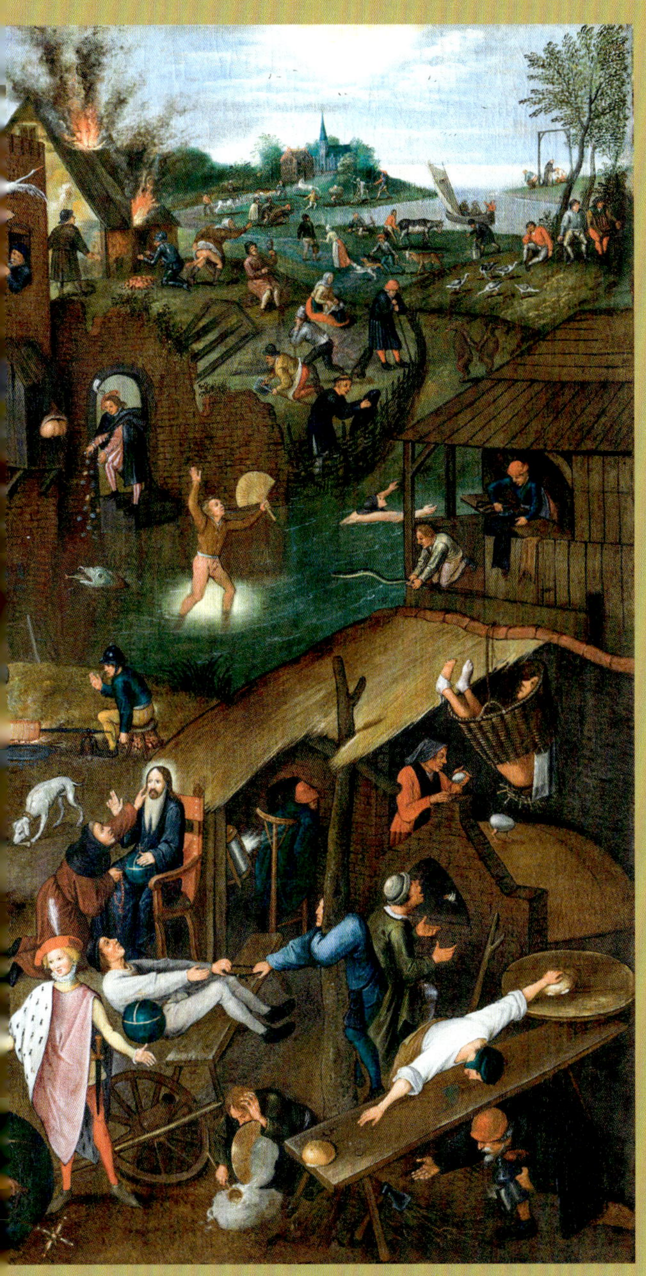

Pieter Brueghel II

Brussels, 1564 – Antwerp, 1638

Dutch Proverbs, *c.* 1625

oil on canvas

Dancing bears, a docile lamb and a man urinating at the moon. If you look carefully, you'll see all kinds of Dutch proverbs in this village. Some are still in use today, others have fallen into disuse. The proverbs are about how to behave, but what we see here is mainly examples of how not to behave. Which is much more fun to look at, of course. Pieter Brueghel came from a famous Flemish family of artists. This is one of the many copies he made of his father's work.

Willem Claesz Heda

Haarlem, 1594 – Haarlem, 1680

Still Life with Half-eaten Pie, 1633

oil on panel

This arrangement looks quite random, with that silver tazza tipped on its side, the crumpled napkin and a half-eaten bramble pie. But nothing could be further from the truth – Willem Heda positioned each object with meticulous care. Still lifes featuring expensive tableware were his speciality, and he had an unparalleled ability to depict different materials, each of which reflects the light in a particular way. Heda needed only a limited range of colours to render the silver, tin and glass, the only colourful highlight being the bright yellow of the lemon.

acquired with the support of the Rembrandt Association

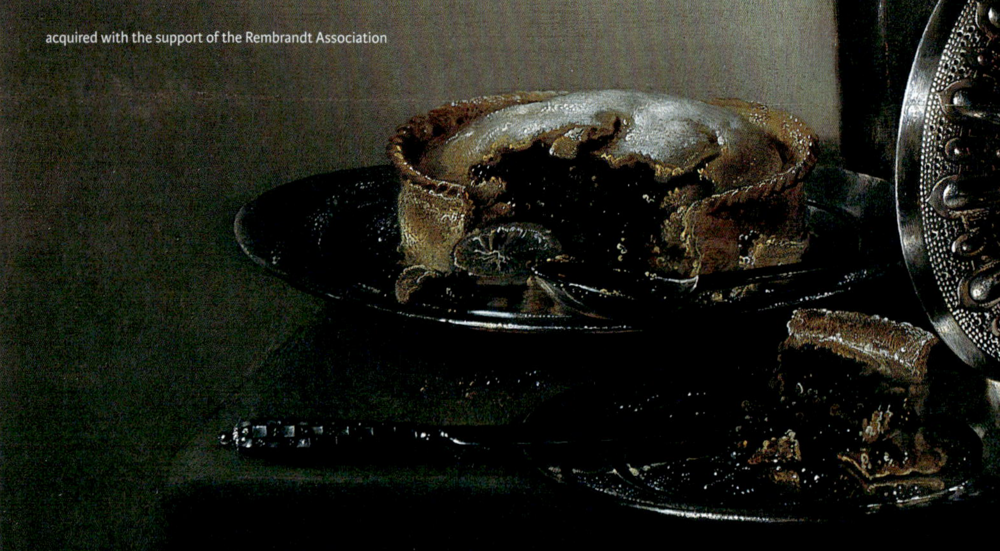

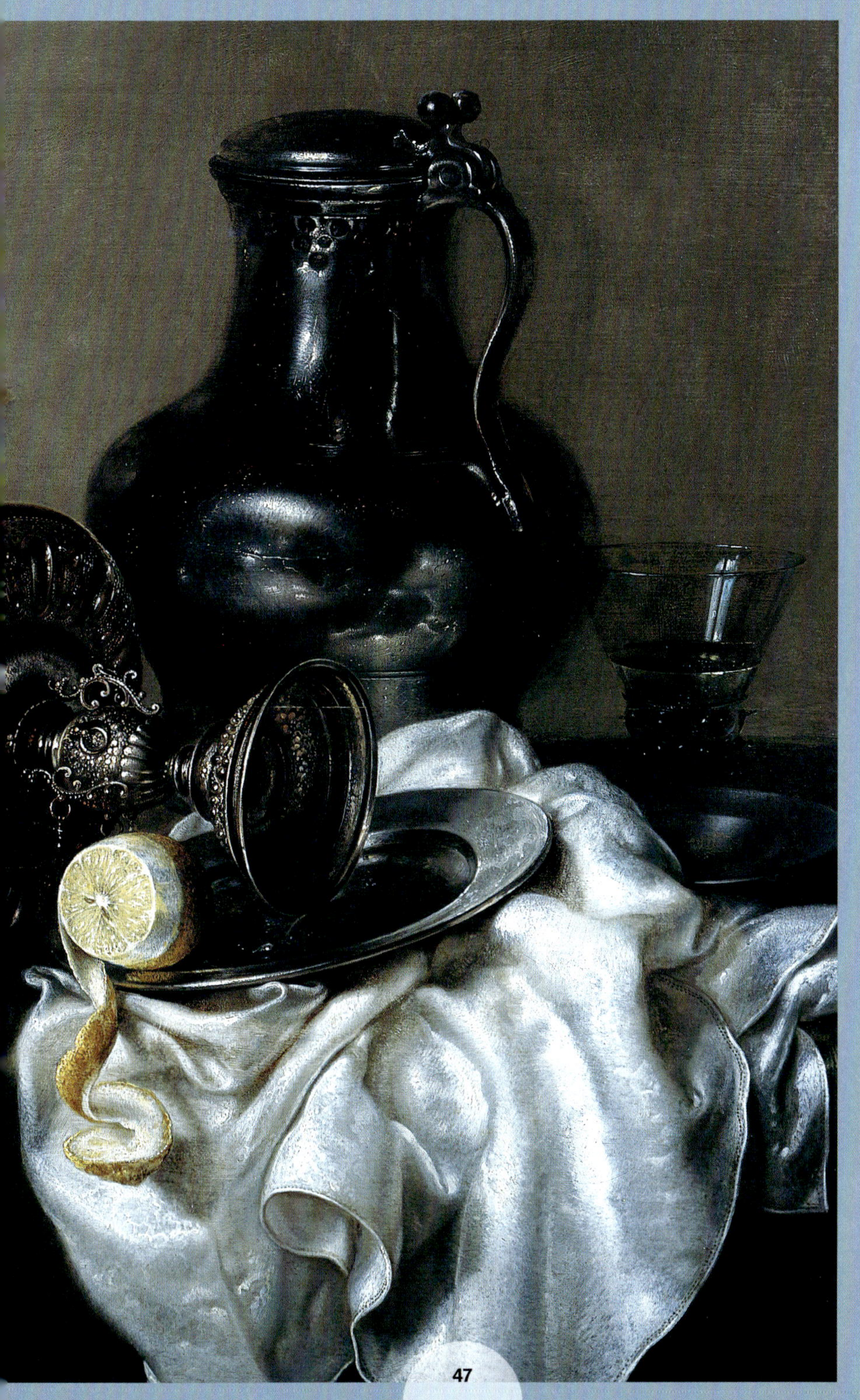

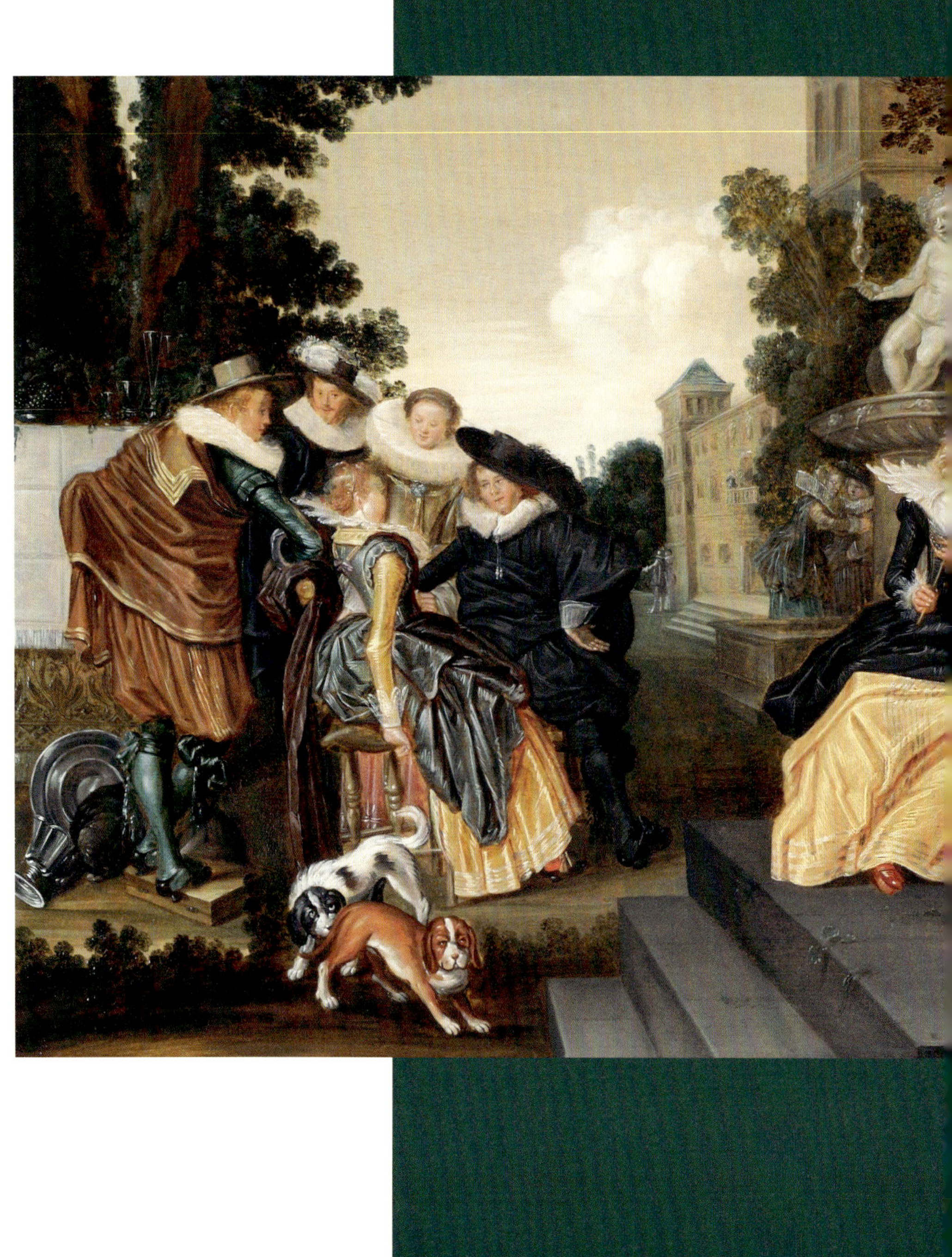

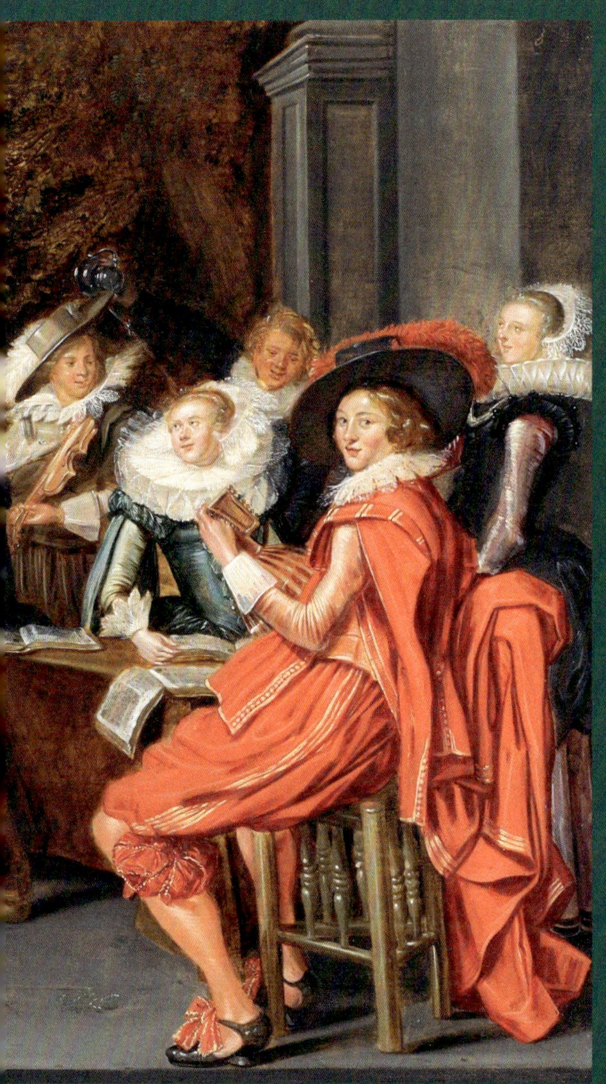

Dirck Hals

Haarlem, 1591 – Haarlem, 1656

Company Playing Music in a Garden, *c.* 1620

oil on panel

A group of young people have gathered in the park of a country house. They are talking and making music, all dressed in the latest fashions. Just look at that scarlet ensemble! Contemporaries would have understood that this painting is all about love which, like music, is more beautiful when there is harmony. But the love portrayed here by Dirck Hals – younger brother of Frans – is not merely spiritual. These revellers are openly flirting. Even the dogs are sniffing each other.

acquired with the support of the Friends of the Frans Hals Museum

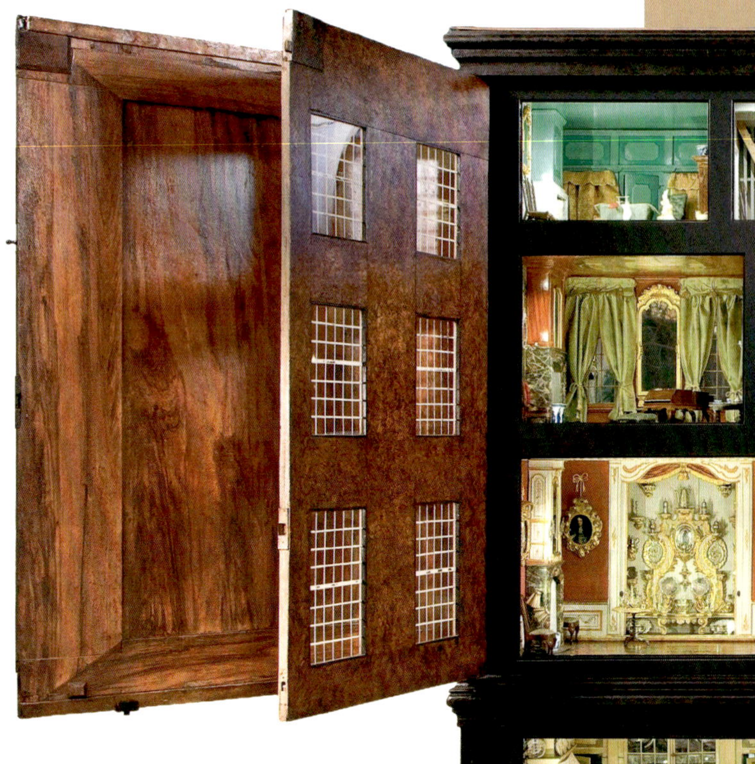

Sara Rothé Doll's House

various materials

In the 17th and 18th century, doll's houses were not children's toys, but an expensive hobby for wealthy women. They were miniature depictions of the ideal affluent household. From the furniture and paintings to the candelabras and crockery – everything was made by craftsmen who also produced such items in a normal size.
This doll's house belonged to the immensely wealthy Sara Rothé (1699-1751). She was married to a merchant, Jacobus Ploos van Amstel, and lived on Amsterdam's elegant Keizersgracht. Rothé had two doll's houses, both of which have survived.

acquired with the support of the Rembrandt Association

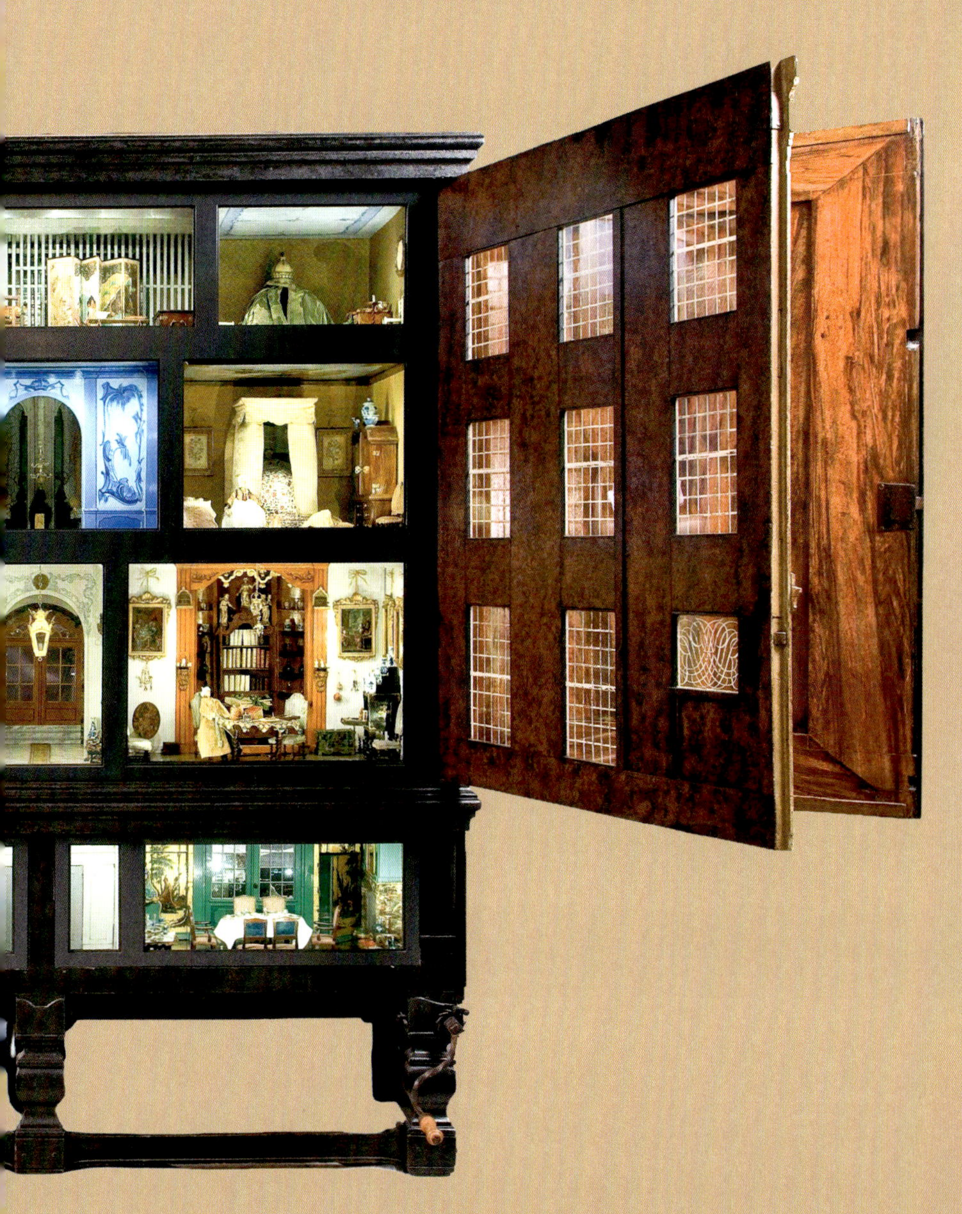

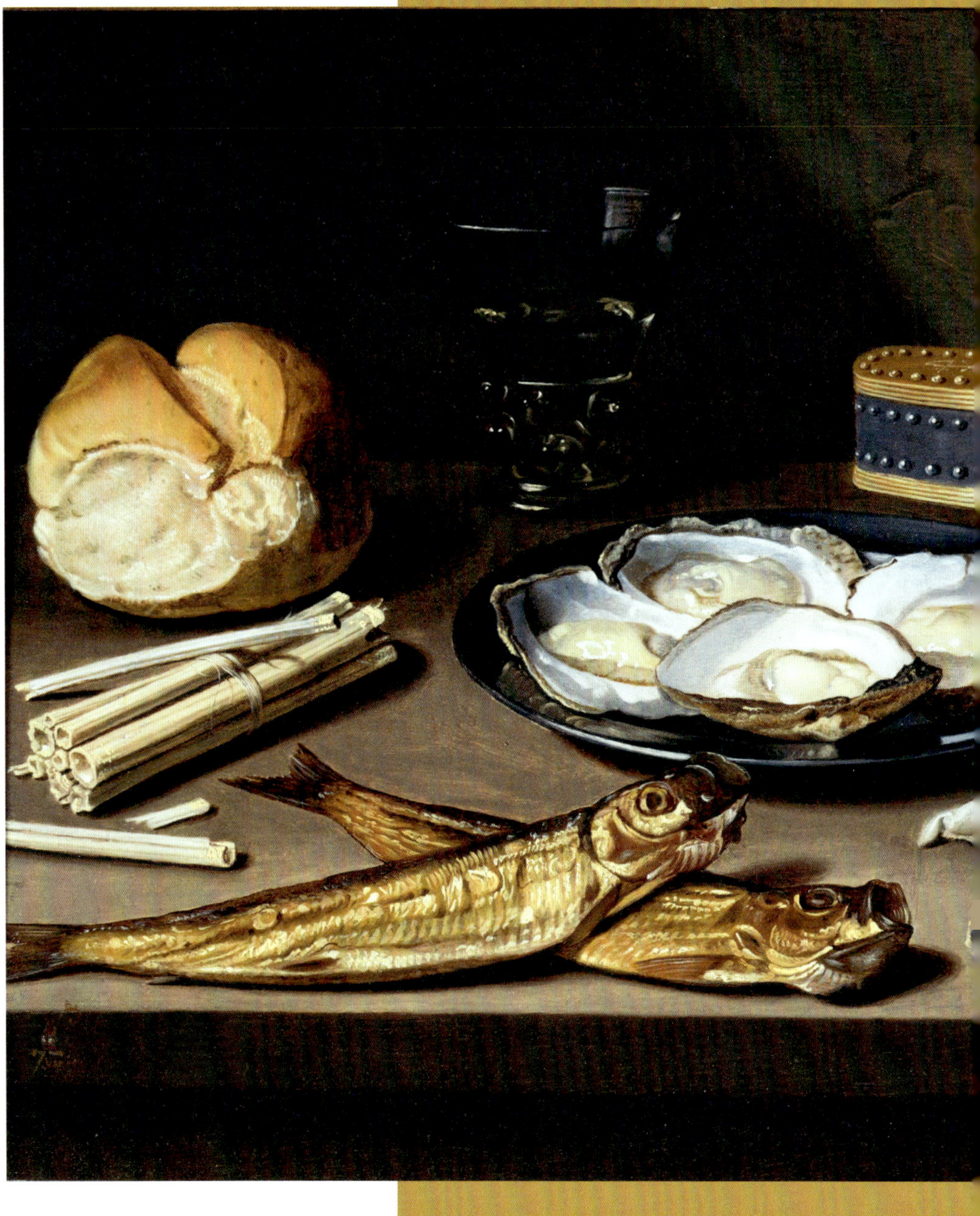

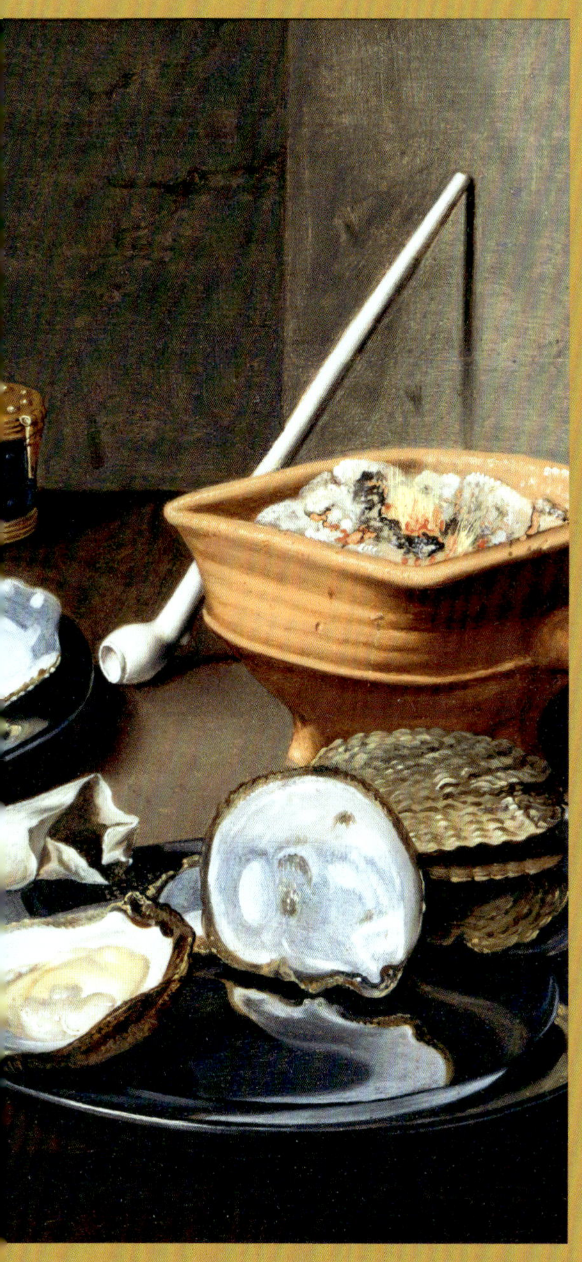

Floris van Schooten

Unknown, 1585/88 – Haarlem, 1656

Still Life with Herring, Oysters and Smokes, *c.* 1625

oil on panel

Two plates of oysters are positioned beside two smoked herrings. Served with the bread and a glass of white wine, this promises to be a delicious meal. Various smoking accoutrements are also visible on the table, including a clay pipe and a bundle of matchsticks. This still life composition gave Floris van Schooten an opportunity to paint a variety of textures, from sparkling oyster liquor to glowing embers.

acquired with the support of the Rembrandt Association and Fonds De Man

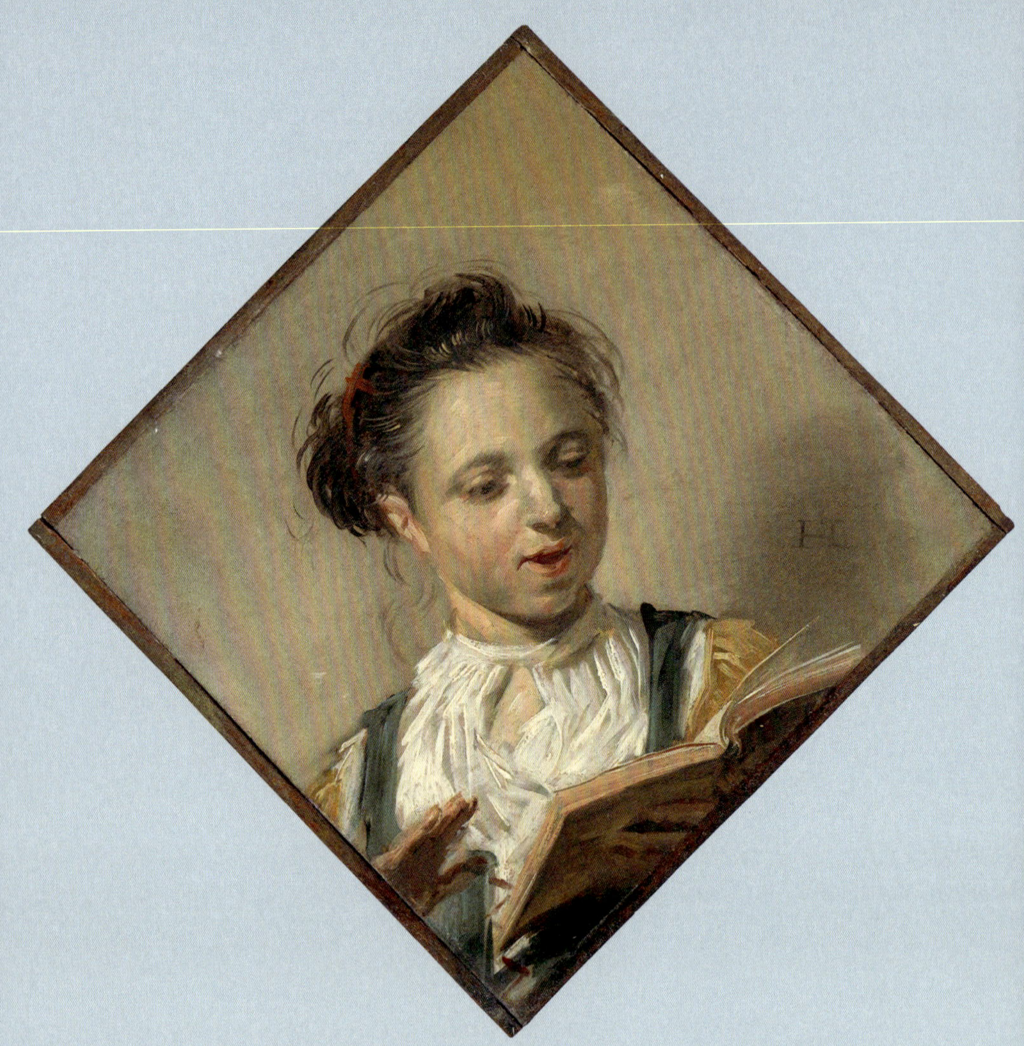

Frans Hals
Antwerp, *c.* 1583 – Haarlem, 1666

Singing Girl and Boy Playing the Violin, *c.* 1628
oil on panel

A girl sings, keeping time with her hand, and a boy plays the violin. You can almost hear the music. Are these perhaps two of Frans Hals' own children, seen through the eyes of their artist father? Hals painted these two small works in his signature loose style, with visible brushwork, despite their size. But they were not intended for personal use. Cheerful images like this were popular, and they sold well.

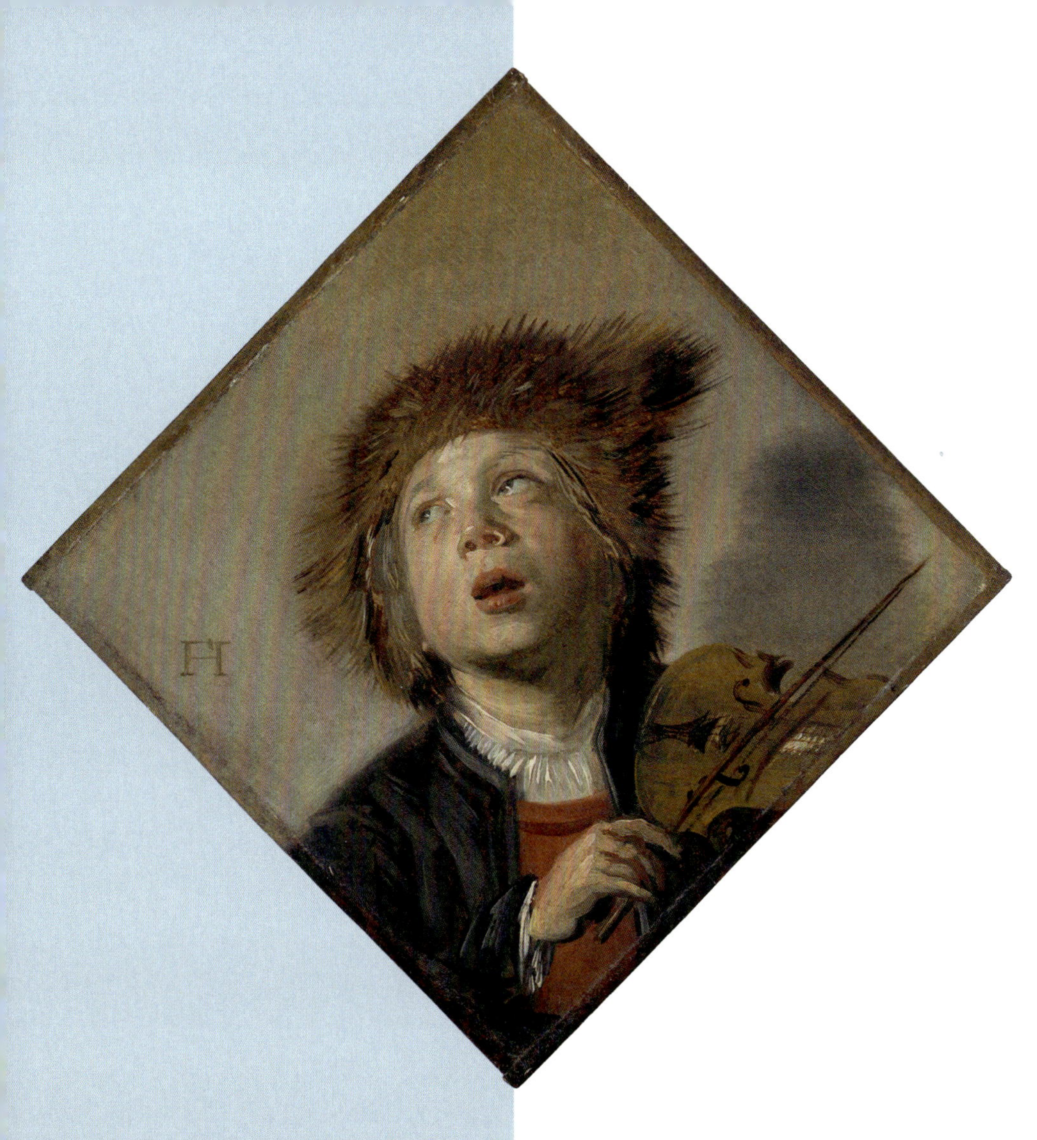

acquired jointly by the Frans Hals Museum and the Mauritshuis in The Hague, with the support of the Rembrandt Association (courtesy of its Nationaal Fonds Kunstbezit, its Dorodarte Kunst Fonds, its Arent Fock Fonds, its Themafonds 17de-eeuwse schilderkunst and the annual donation from the Cultuurfonds), the Ministry of Education, Culture and Science's National Acquisition Fund, the Mondriaan Fund, the VriendenLoterij, the Turing Foundation, the Friends of the Frans Hals Museum, Fonds De Man, City of Haarlem and private donors

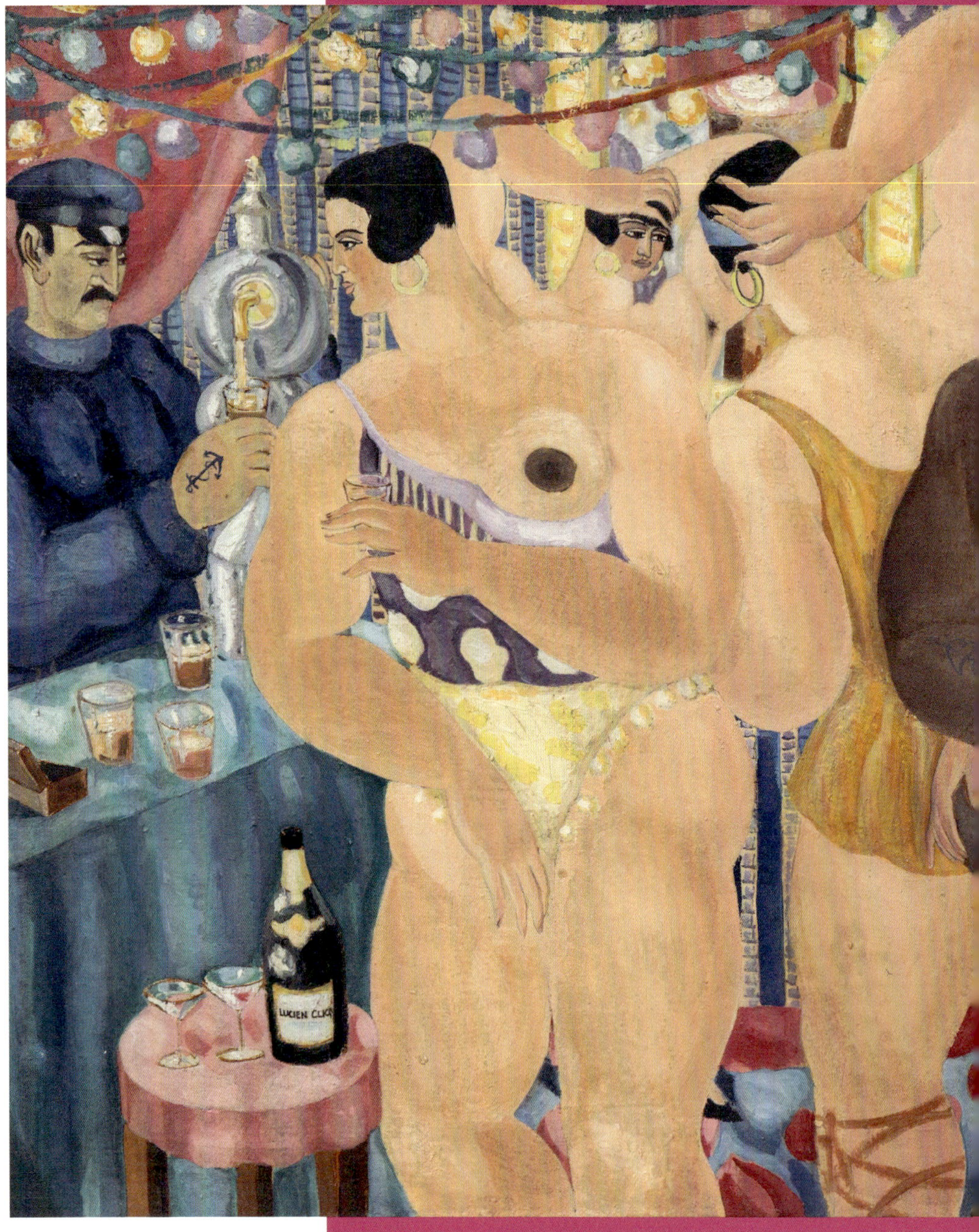
LUCIEN CLIC

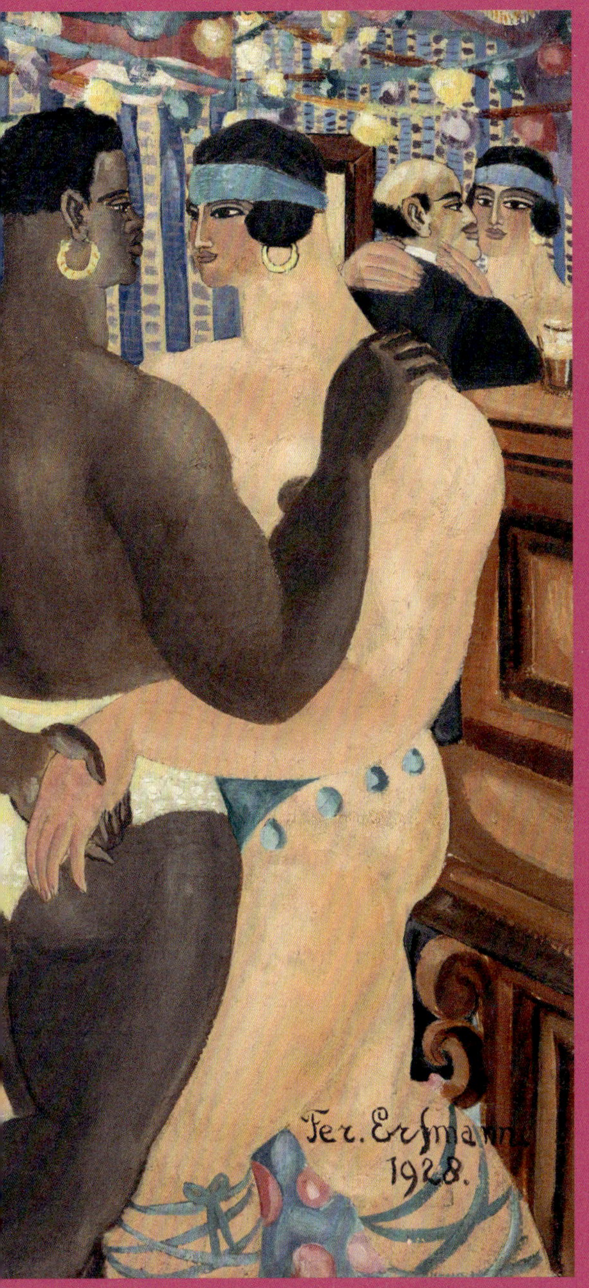

Ferdinand Erfmann

Rotterdam, 1901 – Sardinië, 1968

Bar, 1928

oil on canvas

Ferdinand Erfmann's art and personal life were closely intertwined. He painted mainly at night, often wearing women's clothing and make-up. In his art, Erfmann sought to abolish the strict distinction between men and women, and indeed in this painting, the genders of the dancing figures are not immediately apparent. He may have painted it after visiting Café 't Mandje on Zeedijk in Amsterdam, one of the first gay bars in the Netherlands.

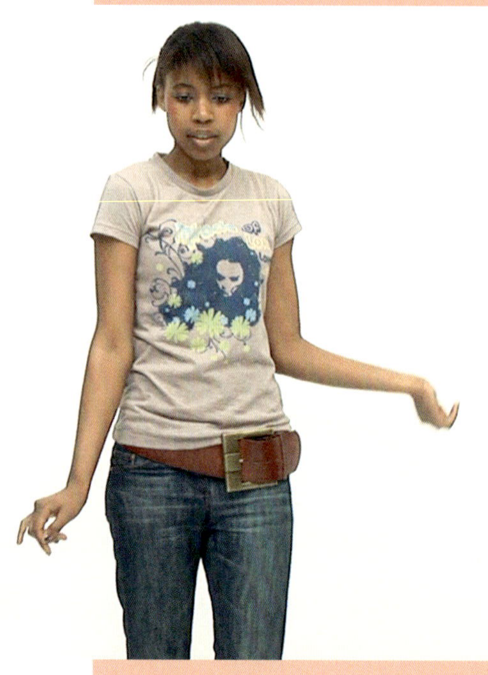

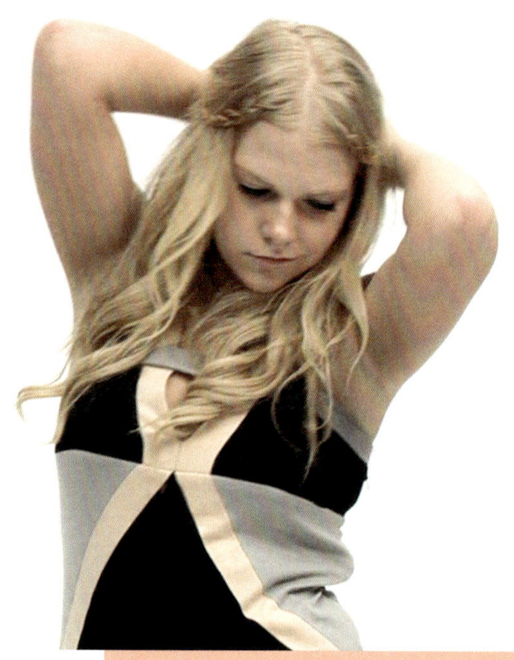

Rineke Dijkstra

b. 1959, Sittard

The Krazyhouse (Megan, Simon, Nicky, Philip, Dee), Liverpool, UK, 2009

4-channel video installation, 32 min

Five young people dance to their favourite music at The Krazyhouse, a club in Liverpool. Some dance with abandon, others are introspective and shyly avoid looking into the camera. Rineke Dijkstra filmed the five dancers in a studio specially built at the club, so we do not see the interior of The Krazyhouse. She was interested in showing how the young people moved to the music, and how they explored their identity, with the associated social and cultural codes, such as clothing styles and dance moves.

acquired jointly by the Frans Hals Museum and Stedelijk Museum Amsterdam, with the support of the Mondriaan Fund

Coba Ritsema
Haarlem, 1876 – Amsterdam, 1961

Still Life with Pink Parasol, 1918

oil on canvas

Haarlem painter Coba Ritsema enjoyed a lot of success with her portraits and still lifes around the turn of the 20th century. At the time, these subjects were regarded as eminently suited to women. Though Ritsema faithfully represented the reality she saw around her, some of her paintings appear almost abstract as a result of the broad brushstrokes she used. The same is true of parts of this still life with a Japanese parasol. Ritsema exhibited the painting in Paris in 1937 at an exhibition featuring only female artists, in which Charley Toorop and Else Berg also participated

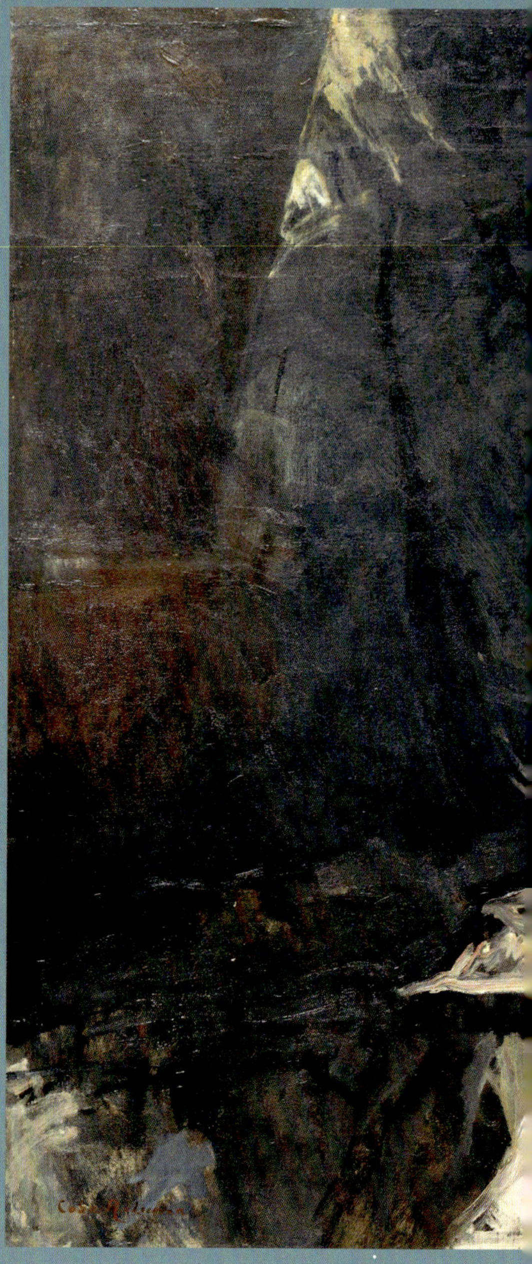

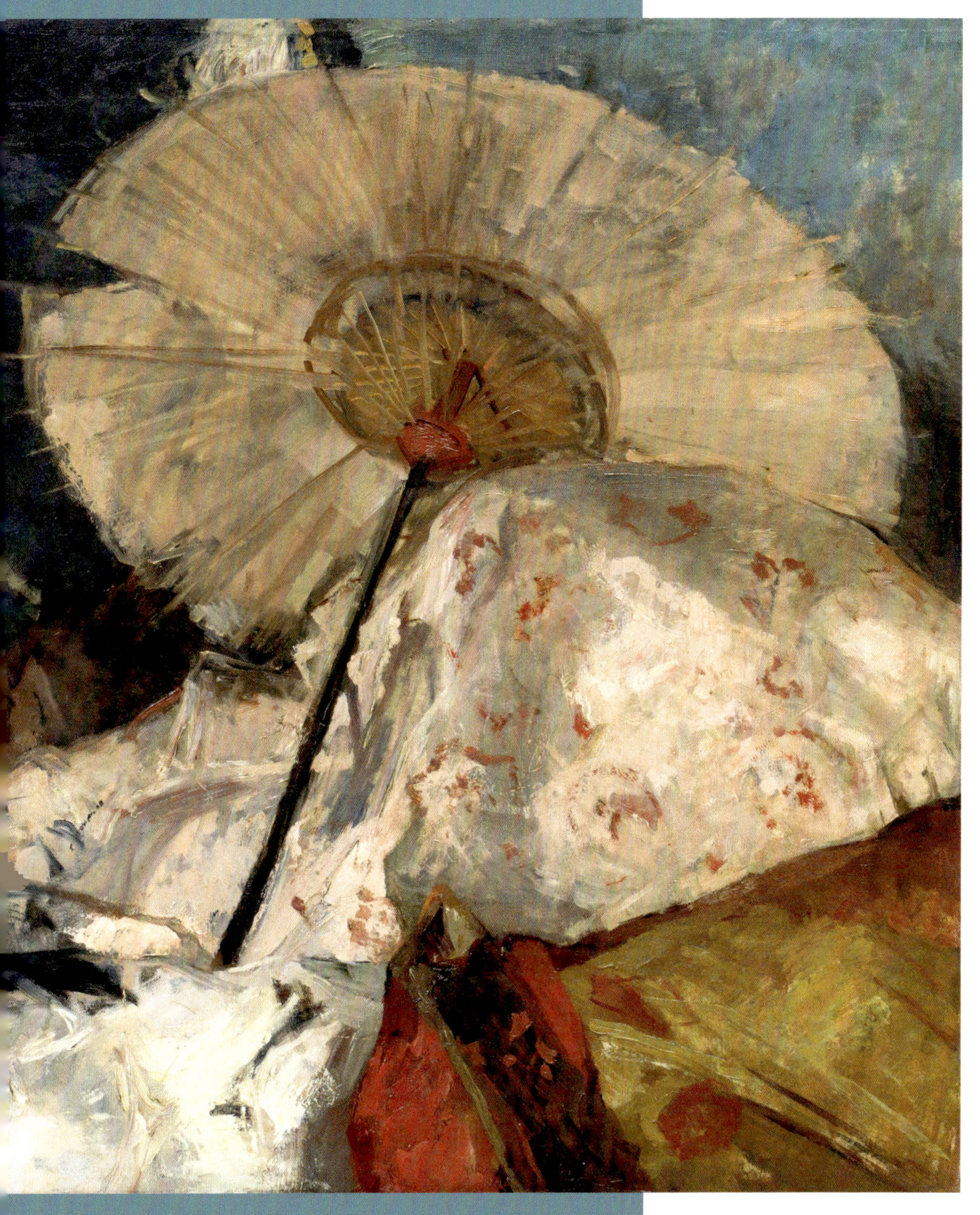

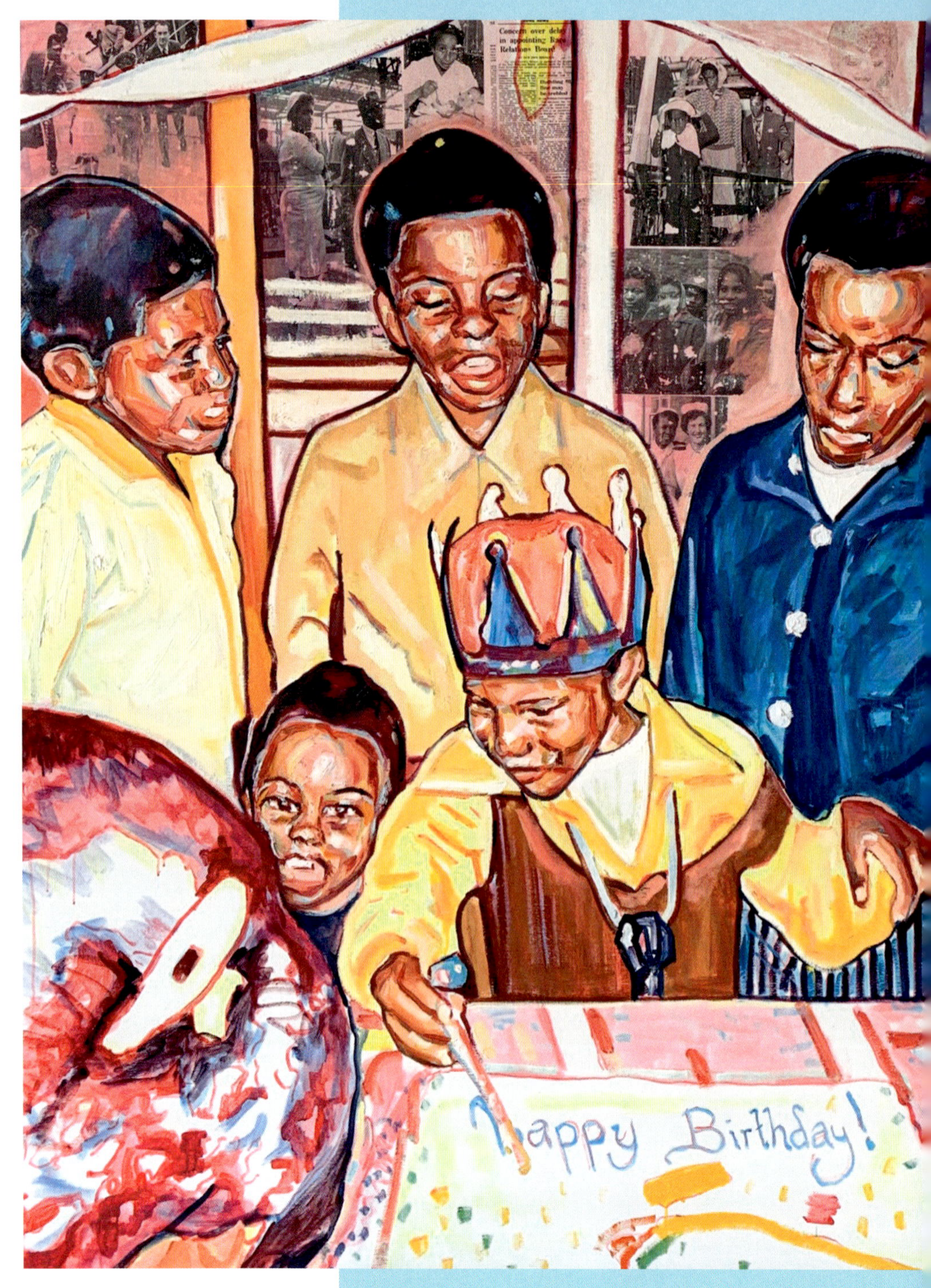
Concern over delay
in appointing Race
Relations Board
Happy Birthday!

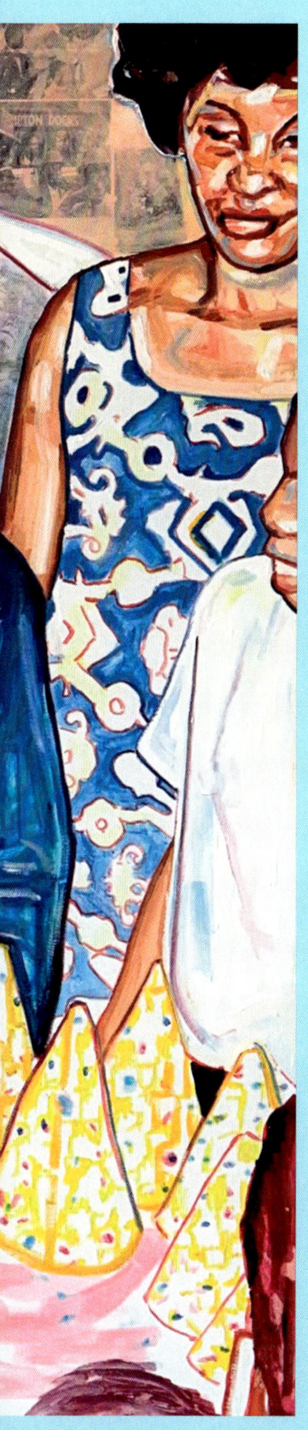

Esiri Erheriene-Essi

b. 1982, London

Having Your Cake and Eating it Too, 2019

oil paint, ink and xerox transfer on canvas

Hurray! - a moment of celebration as the cake is cut at a birthday party. Yet this is not merely a picture of a fun family gathering. In the background are archive images of the Windrush generation, who emigrated from the Caribbean to the United Kingdom at the invitation of the British government after the Second World War, to help rebuild the devastated country. In 2018, the British citizenship of their descendants was drawn into question. The title of this artwork is Erheriene-Essi's way of responding to this. The message: you can't have everything.

acquired with the support of the Mondriaan Fund
and the Friends of the Frans Hals Museum

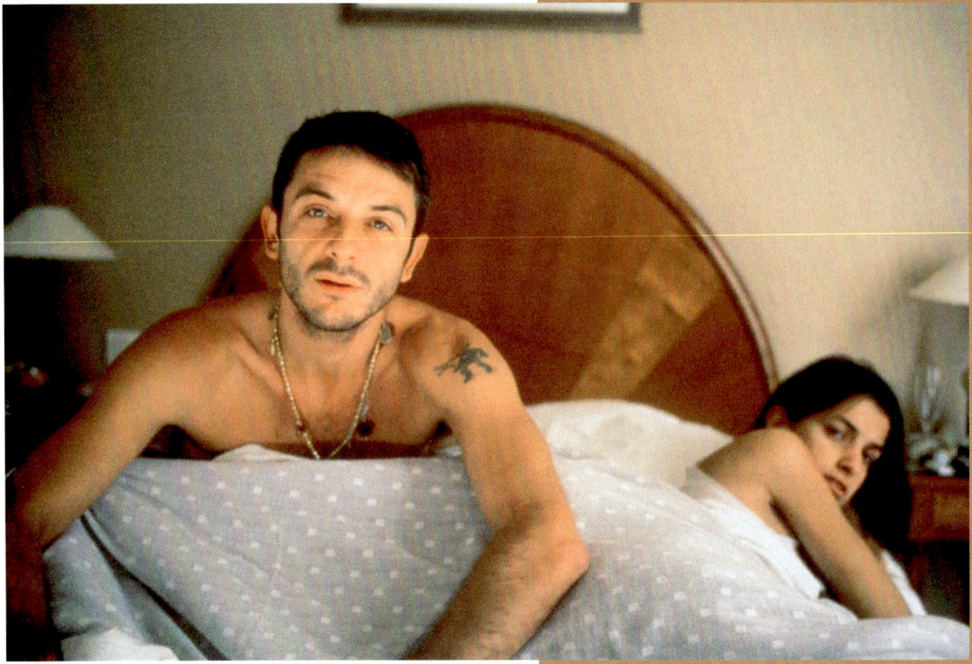

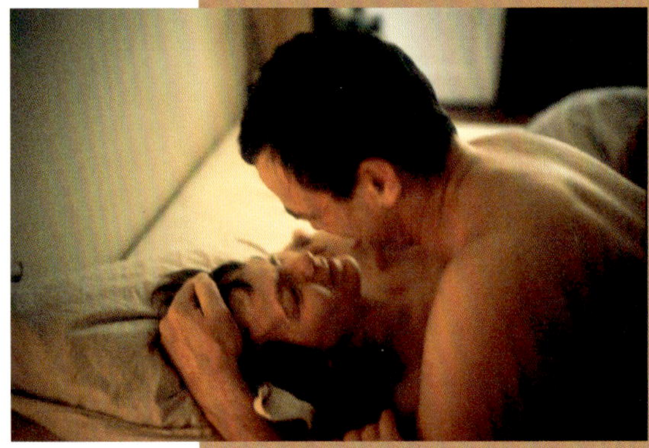

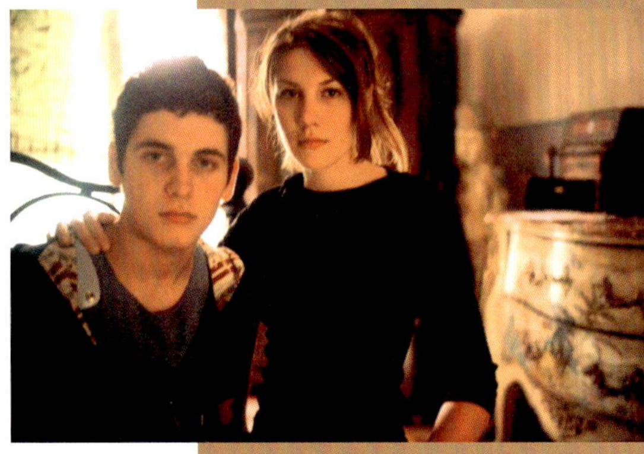

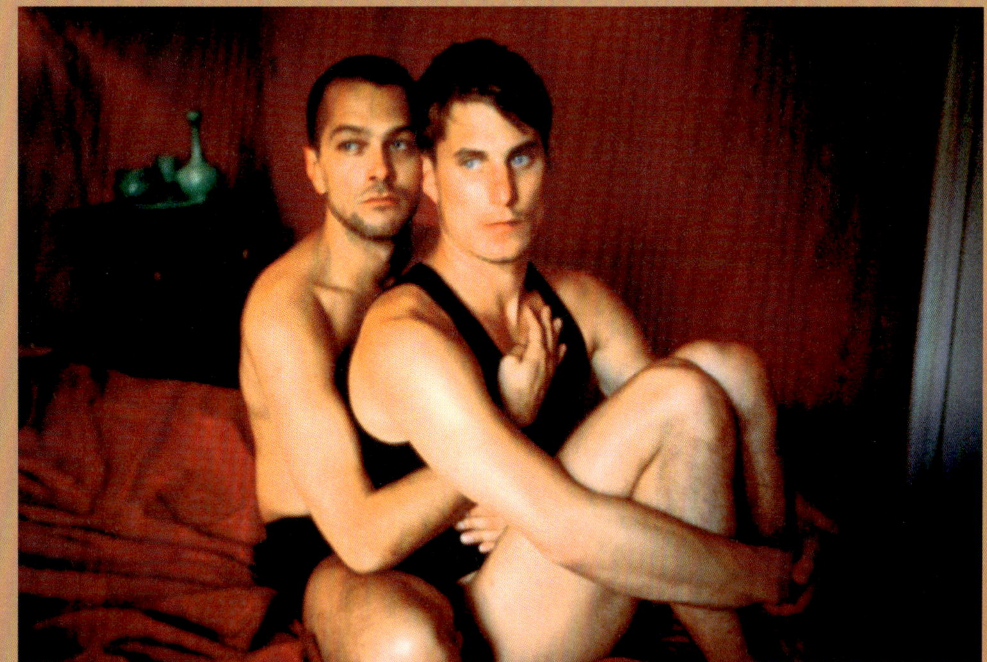

Nan Goldin

b. 1953, Washington, D.C.

Heartbeat, 2001

multi-media installation with sound

American photographer Nan Goldin captured four couples in their most intimate moments, showing Clemens and Jens, Joana and Aurele, Simon and Jessica, Valerie and Bruno making love, kissing and laughing together. Goldin reveals their personalities and their mutual bond. In this work comprising 245 slides, Goldin's focus is not individuals, but people who are intimately connected with each other. *Heartbeat* is a portrait of love.
Goldin often uses her photographs in installations with music. The soundtrack for *Heartbeat* was compiled by John Tavener and performed by Björk.

acquired with the support of the Mondriaan Fund
and the Friends of the Frans Hals Museum

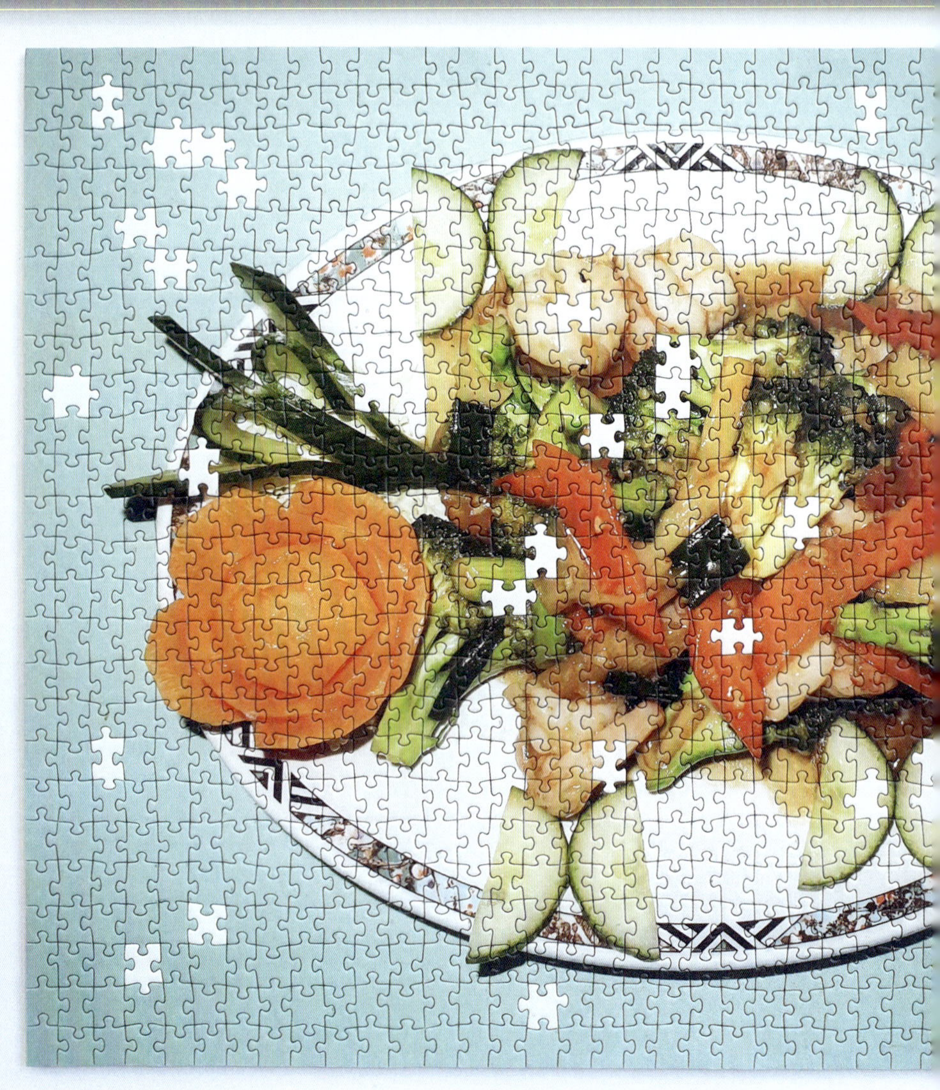

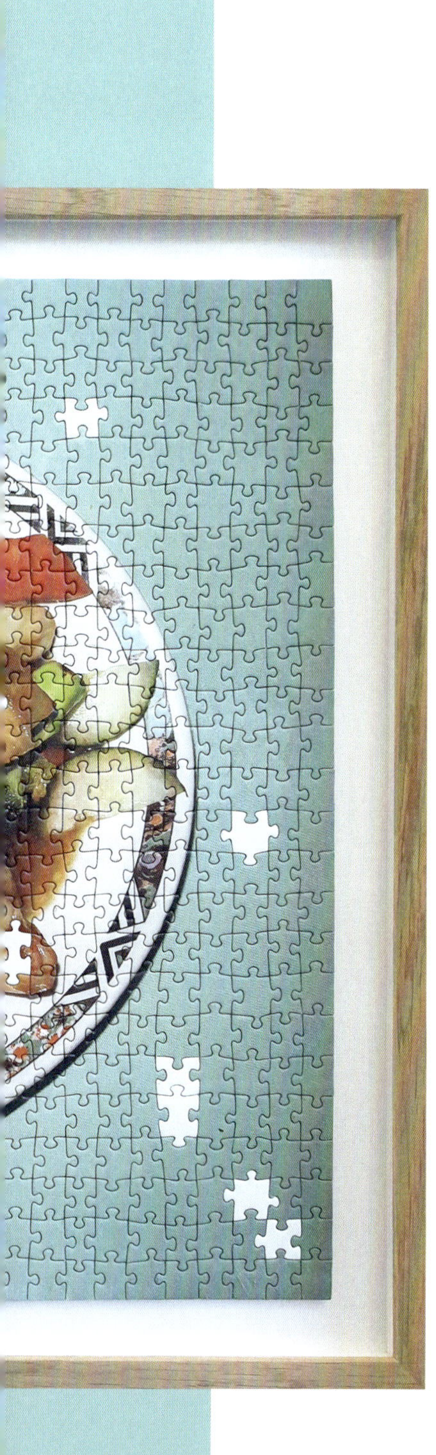

Benjamin Li

b. 1985, Dordrecht

No. 85 with Rice – Prawns and Broccoli, 2023

photograph on jigsaw-puzzle card

Chinese-Indonesian restaurants are an integral part of Dutch culinary culture. They first appeared in the early 20th century, when Chinese labourers came to work in the port of Rotterdam. The Chinese dishes they served changed as people arrived from Indonesia, which for centuries had been ruled by the Dutch.

Benjamin Li photographs dishes at Chinese-Indonesian restaurants throughout the Netherlands, as a way of exploring his identity and family history. Li turns his photographs into jigsaw puzzles, leaving a few pieces blank. These represent the disappearance of the country's Chinese-Indonesian restaurants.

acquired with the support of the Mondriaan Fund and the Friends of the Frans Hals Museum

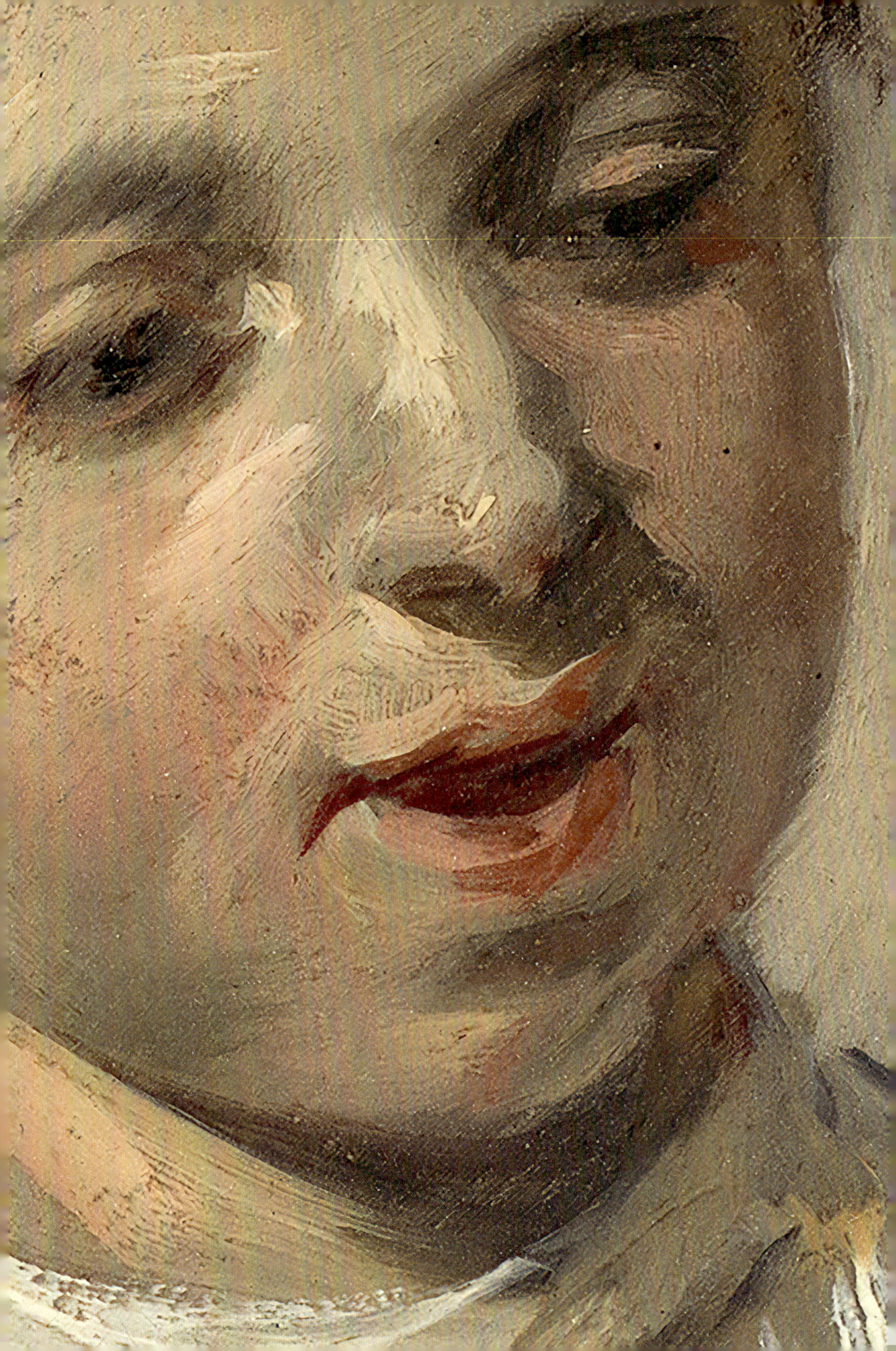

Frans Hals

Frans Hals (*c.* 1583-1666) is one of the most renowned Dutch painters of the 17th century. He produced over two hundred paintings, mainly of Haarlem residents, ranging from small portraits of writers and academics to large group portraits of families, administrators and civic militias. Hals painted them in a loose style that ensured his portraits were full of life. The Frans Hals Museum has fourteen of his paintings, the largest collection in the world.

From Antwerp to Haarlem

Frans Hals was born in Antwerp in circa 1583, the oldest son of Adriana van Geertenrijck and Franchois Hals, who worked in the clothmaking industry. When he was still a small child, the family moved to Haarlem. Frans and his two younger brothers Dirck and Joost all learned to paint early in life, but Frans became the most famous of the three. His career began in 1610 when he became a member of the Guild of St Luke, the professional association of painters. He married Anneke Harmensdochter that same year, but she died only a few years later. Frans remarried in 1617, when Lysbeth Reyniers became his second wife. He had fourteen children in total.

Flesh and blood

The young painter developed a remarkably loose style of painting, which was dubbed 'coarse' at the time. But Hals' portraits are distinctively lively. The subjects are often relaxed, with a smile on their lips, or seem to be speaking. Frans Hals painted real people of flesh and blood such as you might meet in the street. His flamboyant style was popular with art lovers, who were keen to have their portrait painted by him.

Civic guard paintings

Hals' clientele were mainly people from the Haarlem upper class, and included wealthy brewers, merchants, regents and regentesses (governors of institutions). He captured them in individual portraits and in impressive group portraits, including his civic guard paintings. Hals painted six of these – more than any other painter. Five were commissioned by Haarlem civic militias, and are on display at the Frans Hals Museum. The sixth was commissioned by an Amsterdam civic militia, and is at the Rijksmuseum.

Haarlem had two such militias – St George's Civic Guard and the Calivermen Civic Guard – that were responsible for maintaining order in the town. Being part of a civic militia was an expensive business, as members had to buy their own uniform and weapon. Not everyone could afford this, so the militias were made up mainly of men from the upper and middle classes. Their wives, sisters and daughters were not allowed to join. As well as being a force for law and order in the town, the militia was therefore also an exclusive gentlemen's club. Many of the members earned their living trading in beer or textiles, and held administrative posts, in Haarlem itself or with the Dutch East India Company (VOC) or West India Company (WIC). It is therefore likely that they were involved in the lucrative trade in enslaved people.

Laughing

Hals also painted people of lesser means, including actors, musicians and children from fishing families. These images are not usually portraits, but genre paintings (images that show ordinary people doing ordinary things) or 'tronies' (character studies). Hals would often depict these people laughing. Since laughing with an open mouth was not considered proper, 'decent' wealthy people would never be portrayed displaying mirth in this way. Children and people of lowly origins were not expected to know any better, and could therefore be shown laughing. Hals will have been fully aware that his lively brushwork was ideal for depicting their happy faces. Some residents of Haarlem preferred to have their portrait painted in a smoother and more even technique. They would therefore commission their portrait from another artist, like Johannes Verspronck, also from Haarlem, who had a very fine and meticulous style of painting.

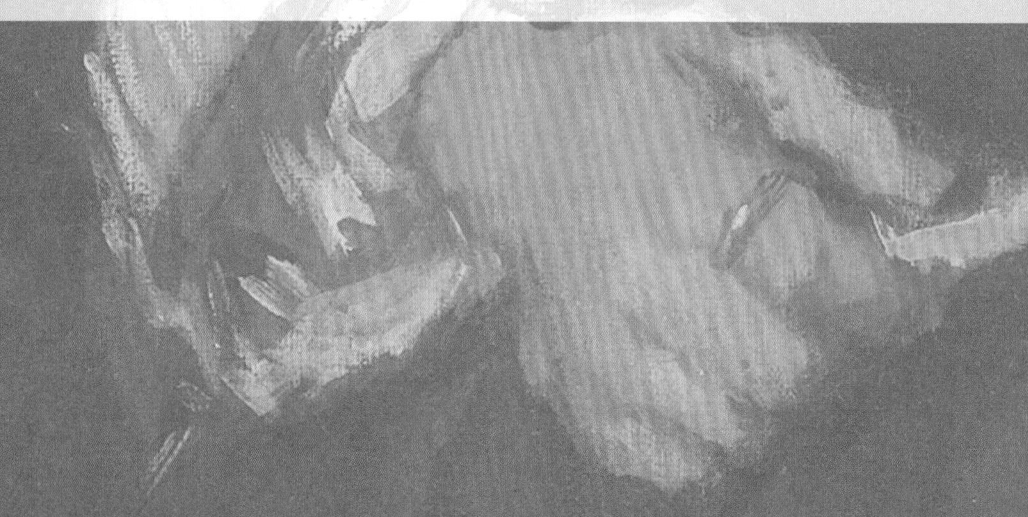

Old age

Though Frans Hals was paid handsomely for his work, he was often in debt. In the final years of his life, he was even supported by the town council, despite the fact that he was still receiving large commissions. They included two group portraits of the regents and regentesses of the old men's almshouse, which he painted when he was well into his seventies. It is remarkable that Hals was still being commissioned to produce work at such an advanced age, as his loose style of painting was no longer in vogue by then.

Grave

Frans Hals died in 1666, at approximately 83 years of age. Since there was no money to pay for his grave, he was buried with his first wife Anneke's grandfather. The grave was however located in a place of honour in the town's Grote Kerk church, also known as St Bavo's Church. Hals finally received a gravestone with his own name in 2021, some 350 years after his death.

Admirers

Hals' flamboyant style inspired both his contemporaries and artists of later generations. The 19th-century painters Claude Monet and James McNeill Whistler were fascinated by Hals' loose brushwork. They regarded him as an exceptionally modern artist and a kindred spirit, and they came to Haarlem to view his paintings. Vincent van Gogh was also an admirer: "What a joy it is to see a Frans Hals like that, how very different it is from the paintings where everything has been carefully smoothed out in the same way." Frans Hals' paintings are still a joy – his expressive style and lively portraits continue to surprise and inspire to this day.

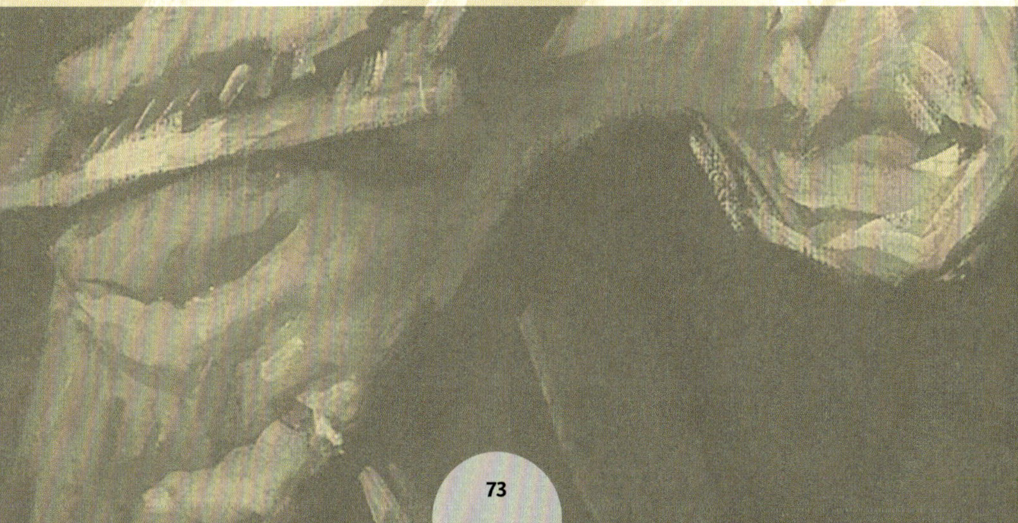

Outd

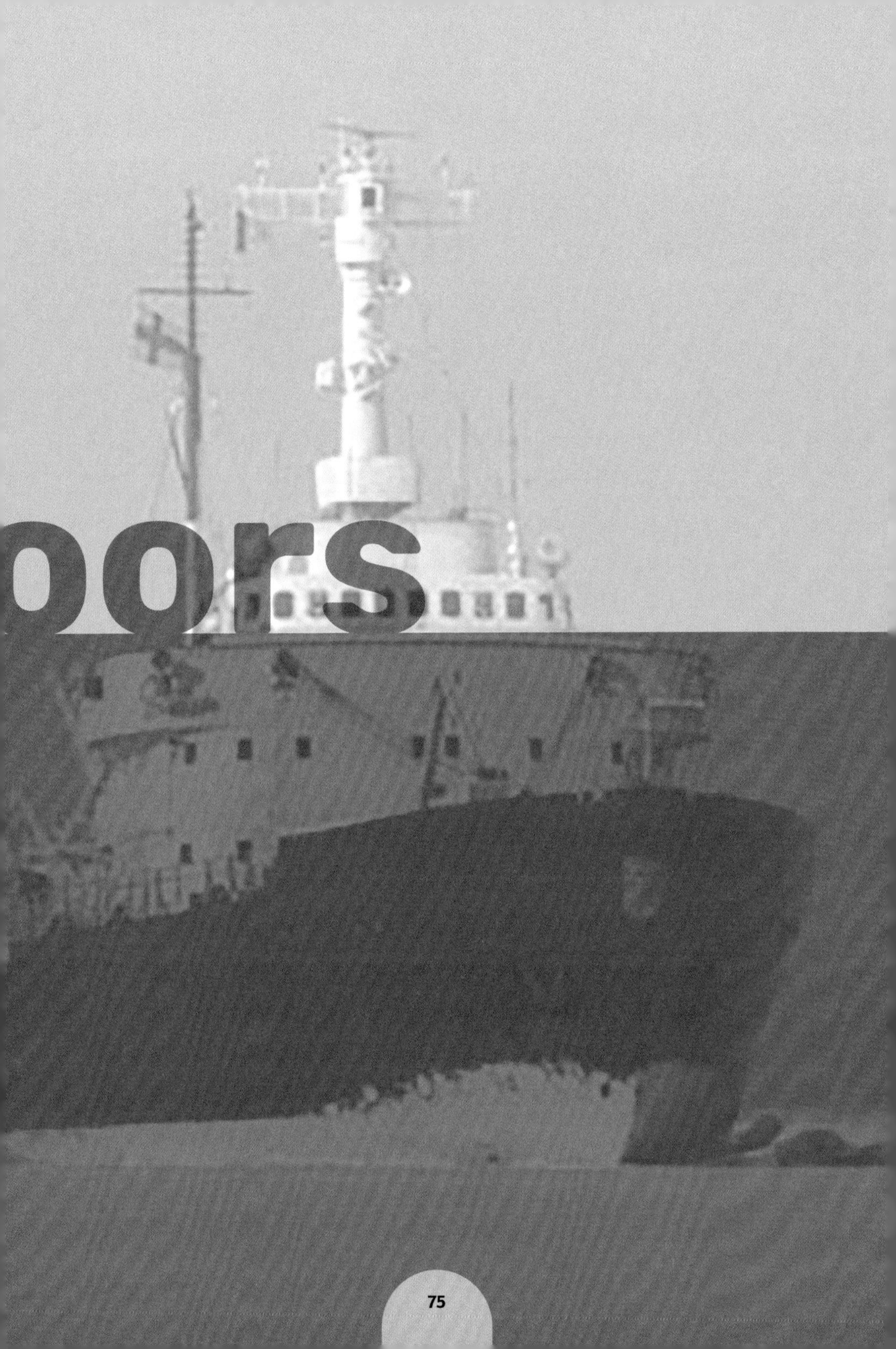

oors

Grote Markt square, the Grote Kerk (St Bavo's Church), the river Spaarne: in the 17th century Haarlem artists loved to paint their own town. Outside the town, they found inspiration in country estates, bleaching grounds, lakes, dunes and the sea. Some artists' main concern was to depict the landscape as accurately as possible, while others were more focused on capturing the atmosphere.

Outside the bubble

The landscape around Haarlem was not the only one subject popular with art lovers. People also loved to buy paintings of those considered to be of lower rank. Scenes featuring drunken, boorish characters at village fairs and in country pubs were entertaining. These images were intended to be humorous, and the contrast with urban life highlighted the latter's supposed refinement and sophistication.

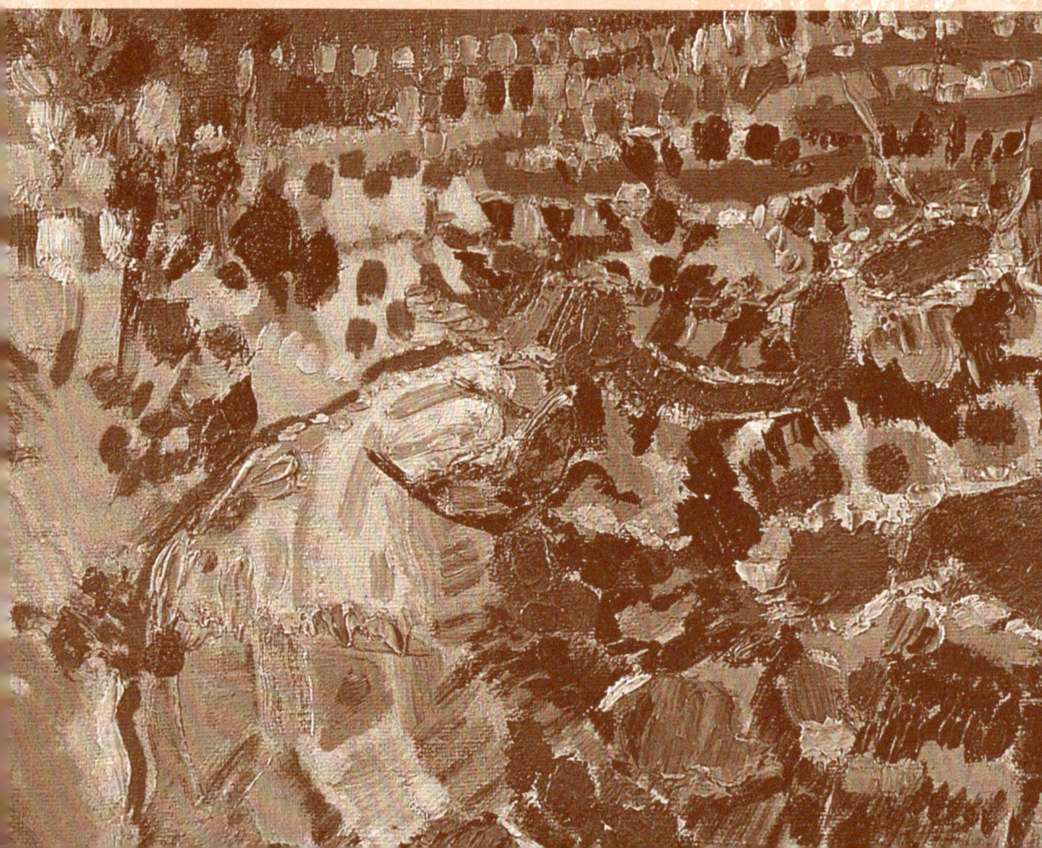

Train and paint tube

Artists of the 19th century also liked to get out and about. In many cases, their interest in nature was a response to the advance of industrialisation, a way of escaping the growing towns and cities with their industrial smokestacks and noisy machinery, in finding refuge in unspoilt natural places. But they too benefited from a whole range of modern inventions. The train made it much easier for them to travel, and with the advent of the paint tube it was now easy to paint outdoors, allowing artists to capture the light and the colours of nature with much greater immediacy.

The wider world

Artists fell for the charms of Haarlem and its surroundings, but there was so much more to discover. So artists also travelled further afield, in the Netherlands, around Europe, and across the ocean. And they still do. The world simply has too much beauty to offer, just waiting to be captured in art.

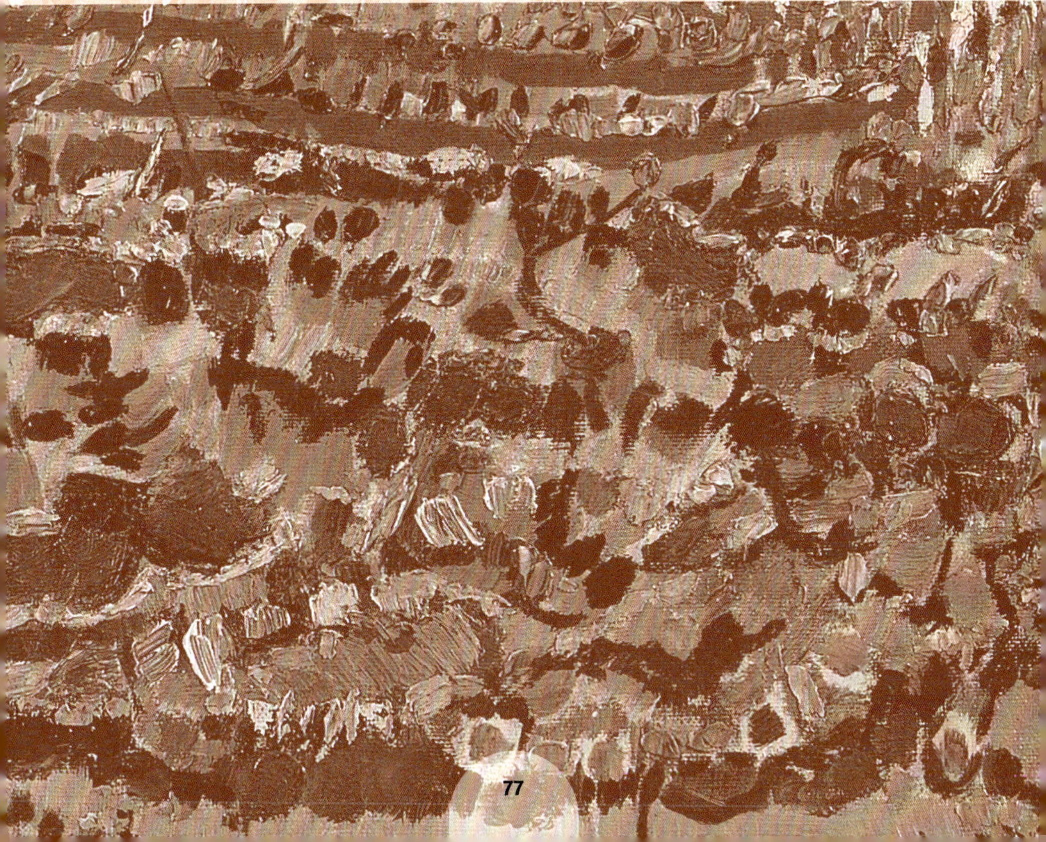

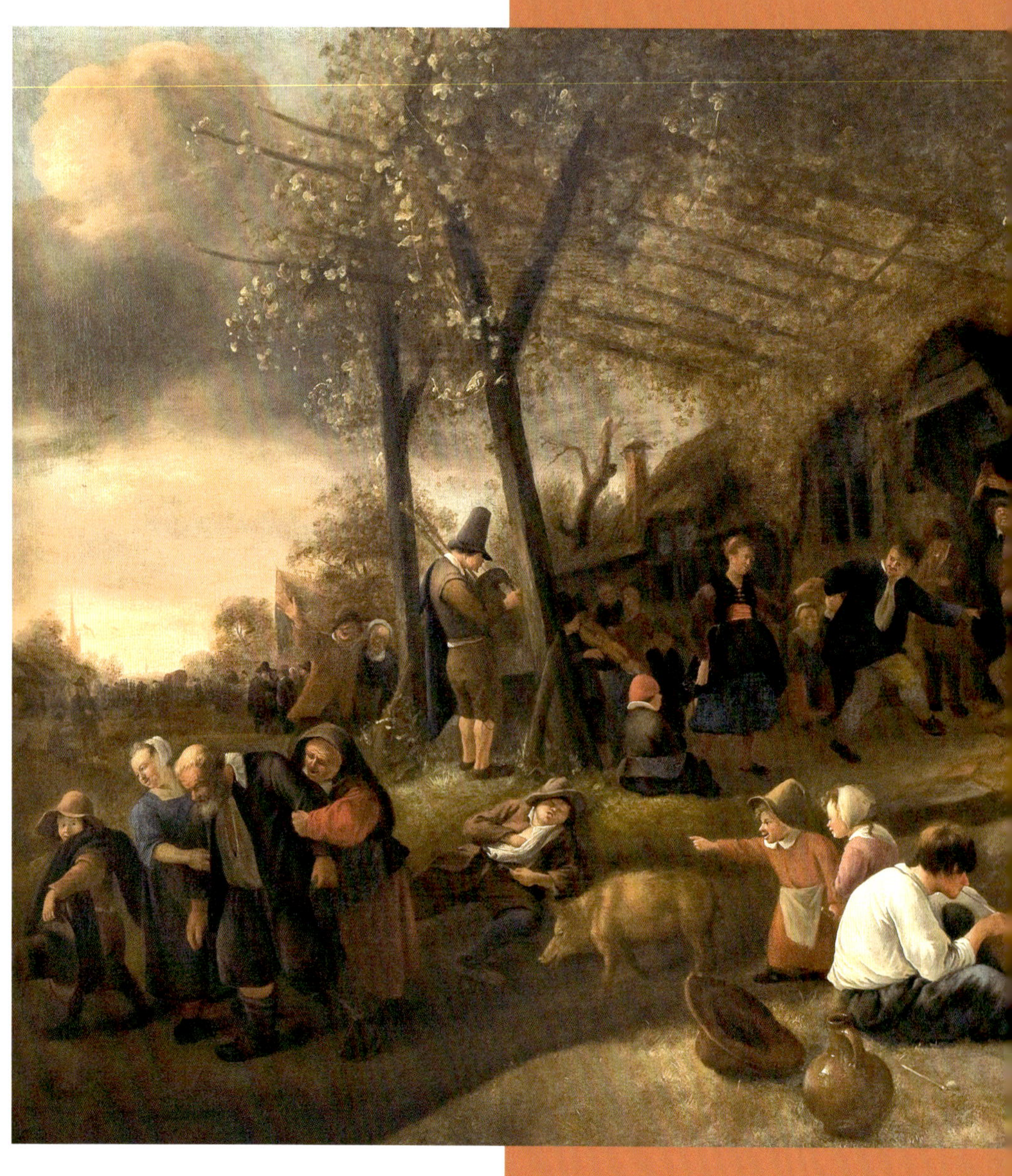

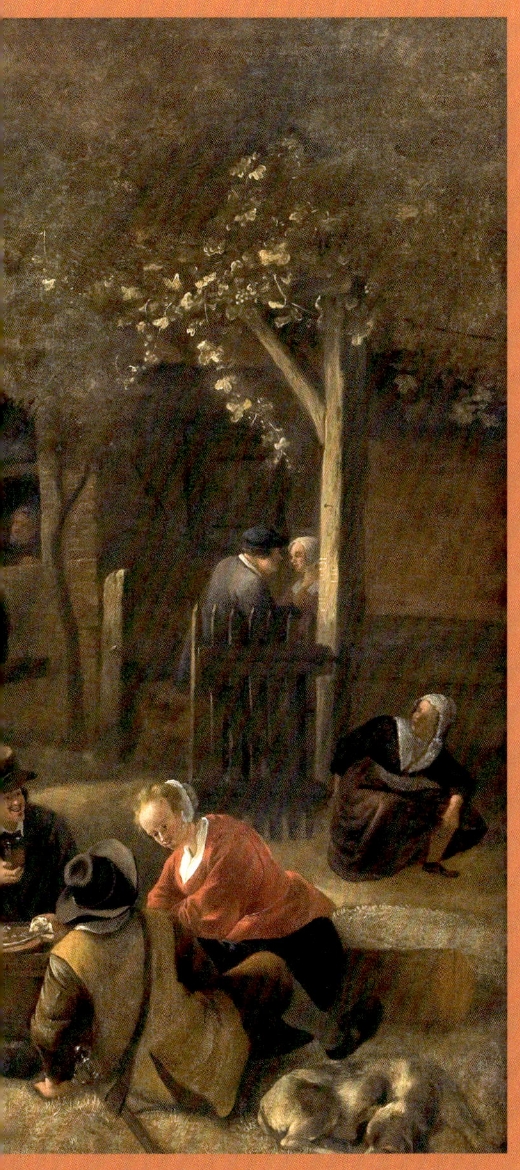

Jan Steen

Leiden, 1626 – Leiden, 1679

A Village Fair, 1668/70

oil on canvas

Villagers play music, dance and drink at a tavern. Two lovers are sneaking off behind the gate on the right for an intimate moment together, unaware that a woman is crouching to relieve herself close by. On the left, a man stumbles home, too drunk to walk upright. Jan Steen painted this village fair while he was living in Haarlem in the 1660s. It was intended as an amusing warning to his audience not to indulge in immoral behaviour. No finger-wagging here, just a gentle admonition.

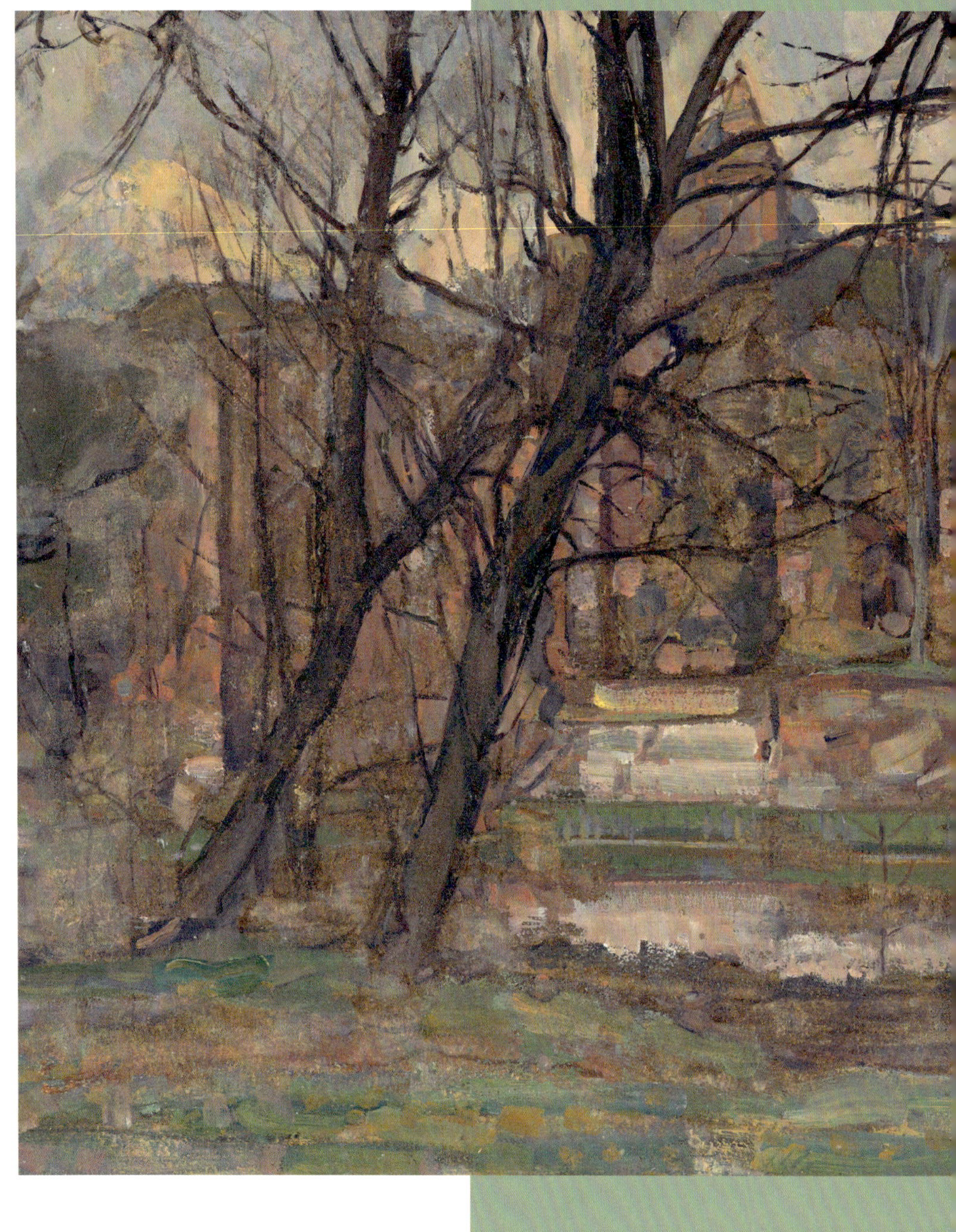

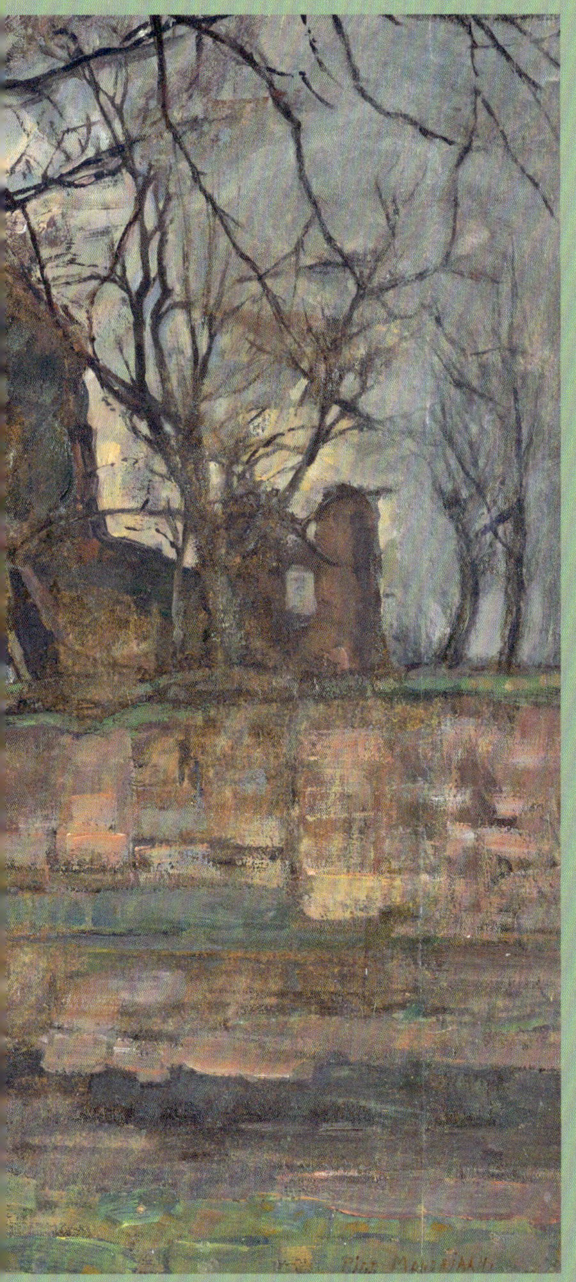

Piet Mondrian

Amersfoort, 1872 – New York, 1944

The Ruin of Brederode Castle, *c.* 1910

oil on cardboard

Nowadays, Piet Mondrian is internationally renowned for his abstract paintings with rectangles in primary colours and black lines. But before he took the step towards this new art, landscapes were his main subject. They included this image of the ruin of the medieval castle in Brederode, near the village of Santpoort-Zuid in Noord-Holland. Mondrian painted it using short, angular brushstrokes, in an early indication of his fascination with geometric composition, long before he made his first abstract painting.

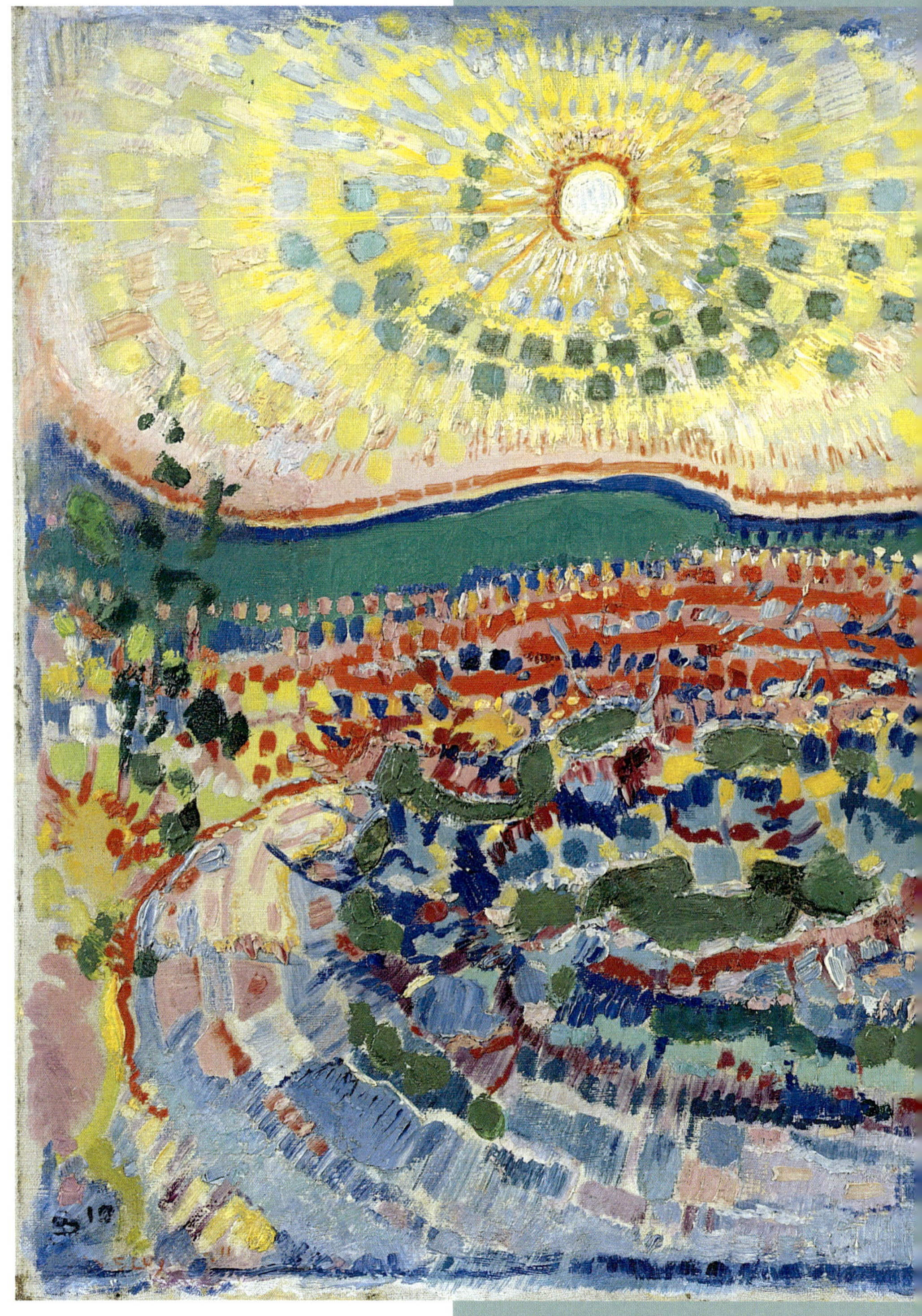

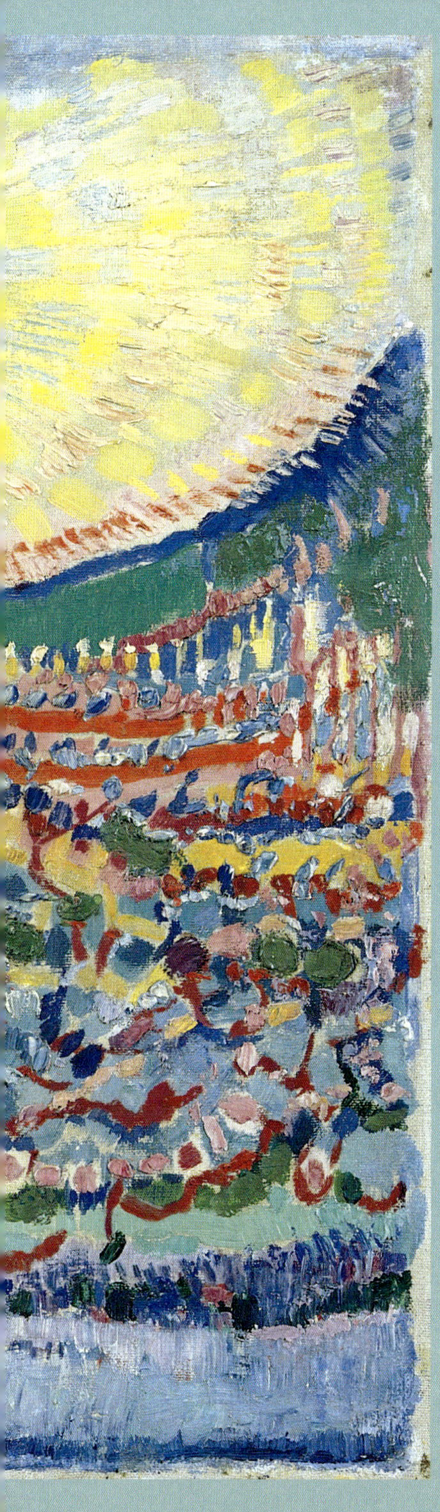

Jan Sluijters

Den Bosch, 1881 – Amsterdam, 1957

October Sun, Laren, 1910

oil on canvas

Sunlight falls like multicoloured confetti over this Laren landscape. The scene is not meant to be an accurate representation – Jan Sluijters was trying to capture the feeling that the light aroused. “If I wanted to paint the sun in a landscape, I would start by turning my back on that landscape and then, after feeling the sensation evoked in me by the light of the sun, I would start composing in yellows and blues and greens.”

Guido van der Werve

b. 1977, Papendrecht

Number eight, everything is going to be alright, 2007

video, 10:10 min

A lonely figure tempts fate, surrendering himself to the forces of nature in northern Finland. He walks ten metres in front of a huge icebreaker, stoically persisting – his eyes on a distant horizon – as the ice cracks beneath his feet. The plodding figure is artist Guido van der Werve, the maker of *Number eight*. He often plays the lead in his films.

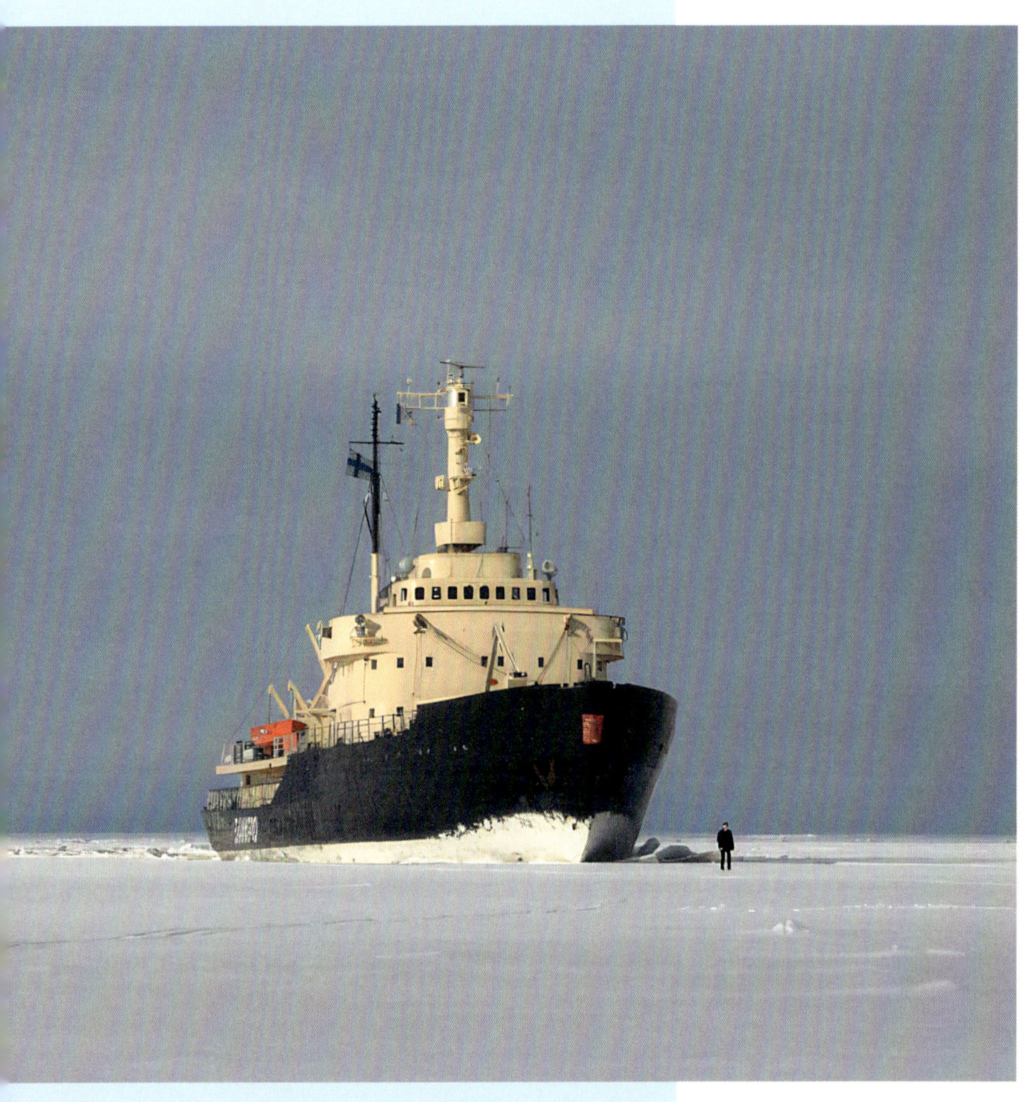

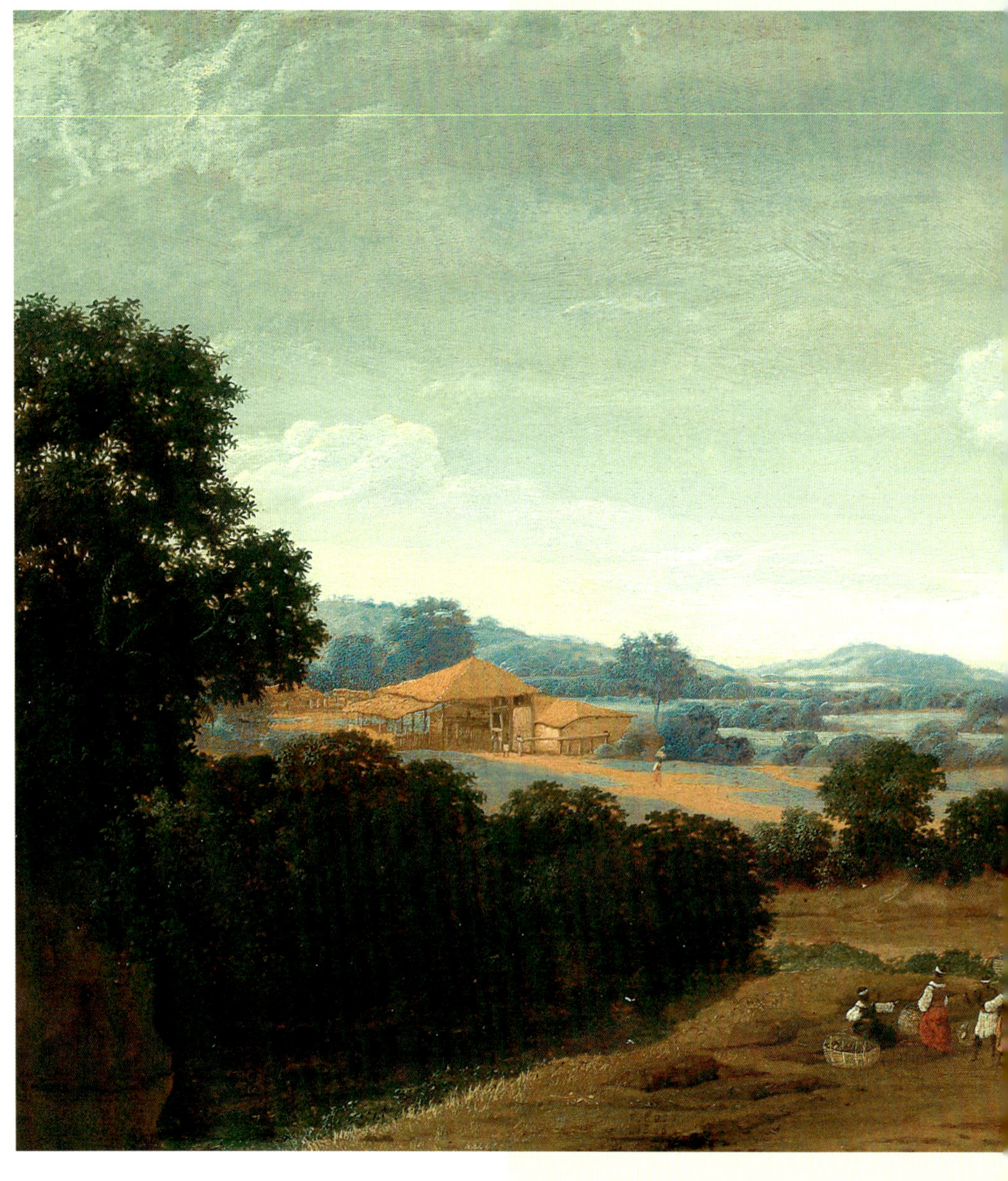

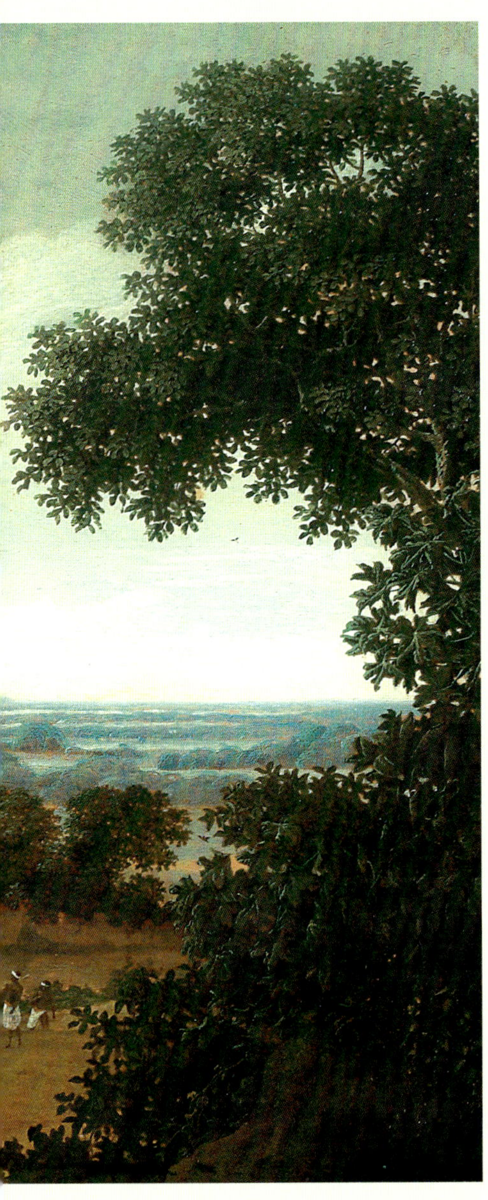

Frans Post

Haarlem, 1612 – Haarlem, 1680

Brazilian Landscape, 1656

oil on panel

In 1637 Frans Post travelled to Brazil, where there was a Dutch colony. There he made a pictorial record of the landscape, the people and the natural environment. Later, back in Haarlem, Post continued painting Brazilian landscapes, which were popular with buyers. Yet these idyllic scenes never showed the oppression of the indigenous people, or the way the Dutch forced enslaved men, women and children to work on the plantations, consigning many to an early death.

Gerrit Berckheyde

Haarlem, 1638 – Haarlem, 1698

Grote Markt with the Town Hall, 1671

oil on canvas on panel

As a young artist, Gerrit Berckheyde painted all kinds of subjects, but from around 1660, he specialized in townscapes, particularly views of Haarlem. The effect of light is always the main focus of his work. Note how the light rakes the façade of the town hall and how the decorative features cast shadows on the wall. The buildings to the left are also part of Berckheyde's thrilling interplay of sunlight and shadow.

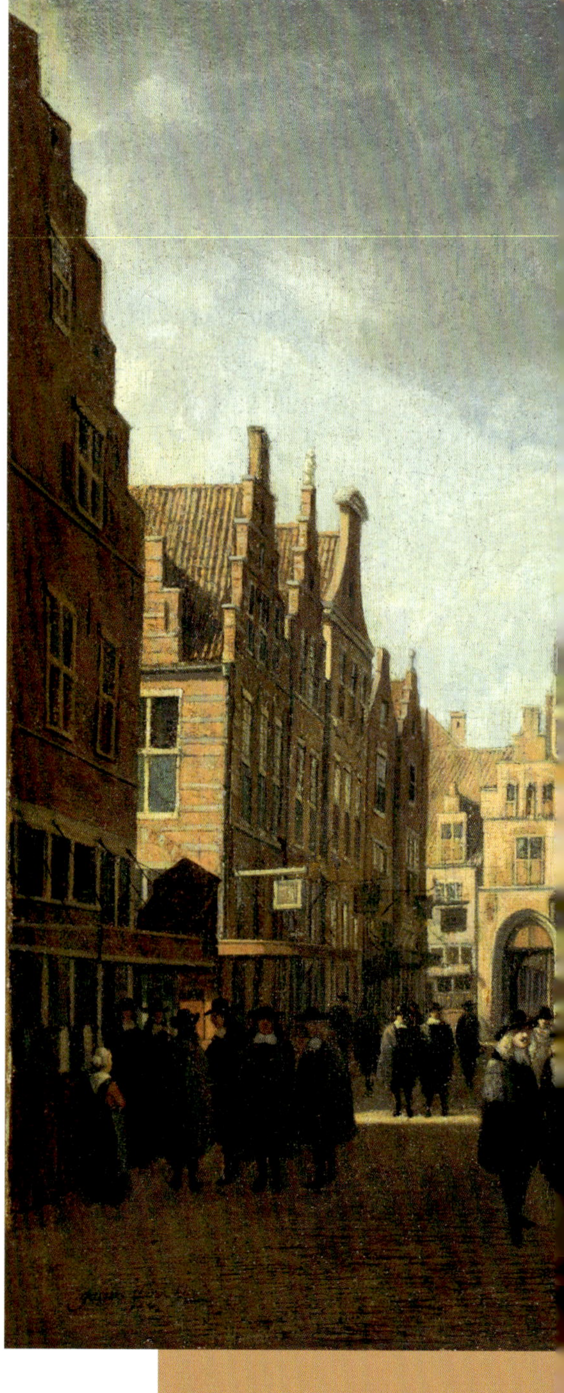

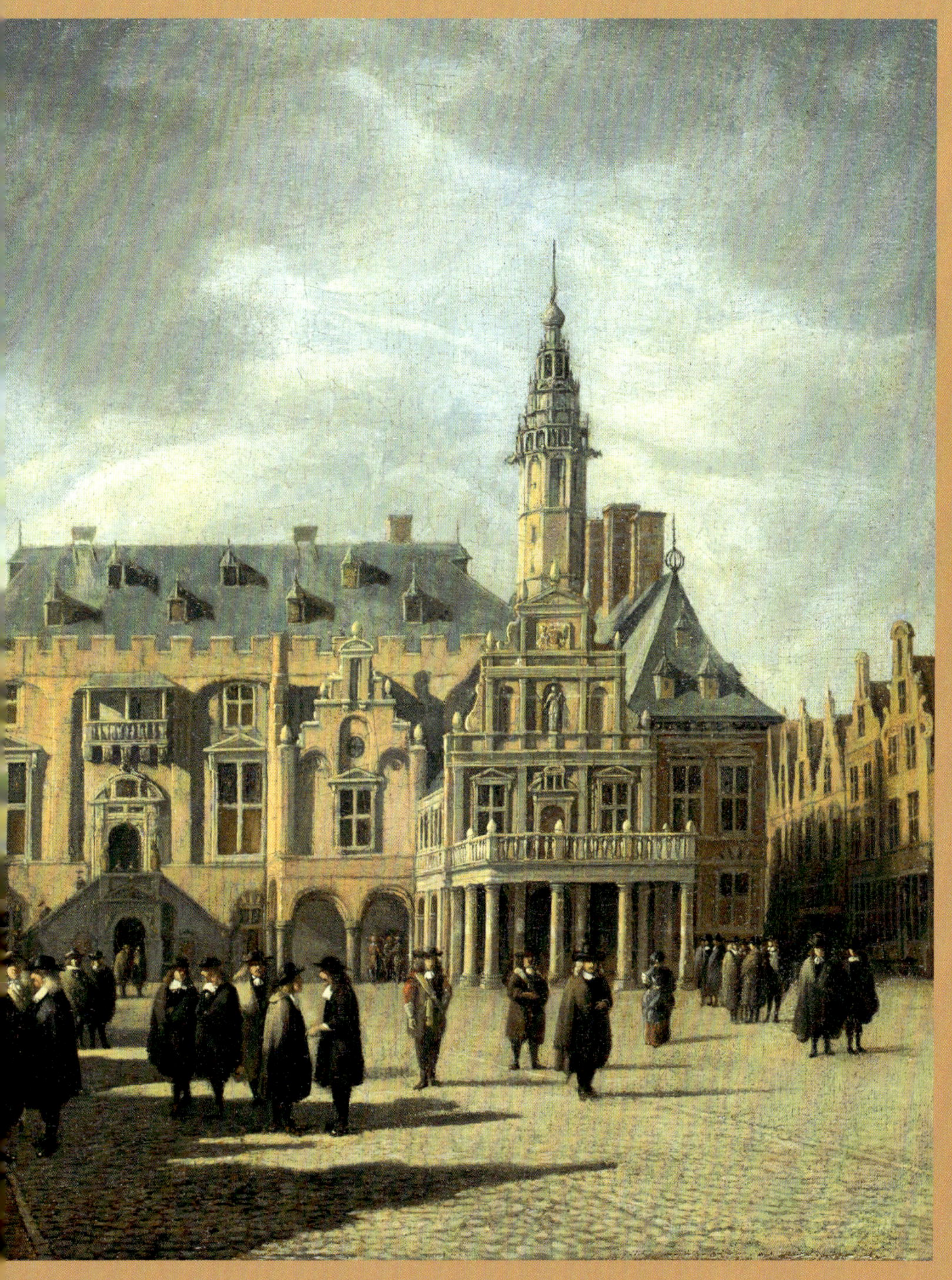

Great

Stories

For a long time, narrative images were the ultimate in painting, the ideal way for an artist to showcase all their skills. An artist had to be able to render people and animals, as well as objects made of different materials. They also had to depict buildings and landscapes, and know the rules of perspective. But the most important goal was to understand and convincingly portray the protagonists' emotions, so that the story was conveyed to the viewer.

The Bible

For a long time, the Bible was the main source of stories for paintings. Religious images helped the faithful to understand the Bible, and to follow the correct path in life. Churches, monasteries and guilds commissioned large altarpieces. Wealthy citizens commissioned small religious paintings for their homes, to show how devout they were, and how much money they had.

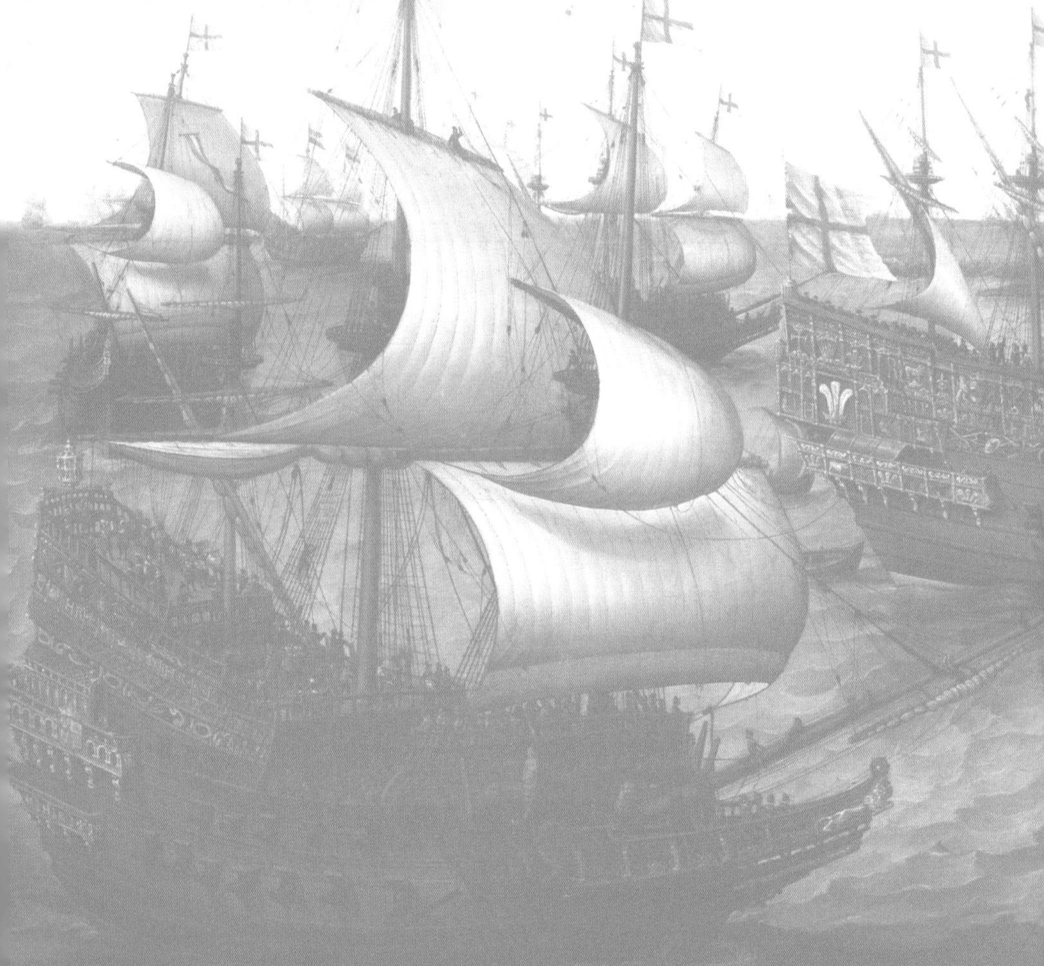

Classical antiquity

But artists had other sources of inspiration, too. In the 16th century, artists and their clients developed a growing interest in the stories of classical antiquity, populated by gods, heroes and ordinary mortals. These stories were often about lust and love, which provided a good opportunity to depict naked bodies. Haarlem artists were very skilled at this, particularly in the 17th century. Depicting stories – with or without nudity – remained an important part of an artist's training in the centuries that followed.

Untold and unseen

Artists also found stories closer to home, including episodes from the history of their town or country. Yet many stories remained untold. Contemporary artists like patricia kaersenhout are increasingly opting to tell these stories in their art, shining a spotlight on people who have hitherto remained unseen.

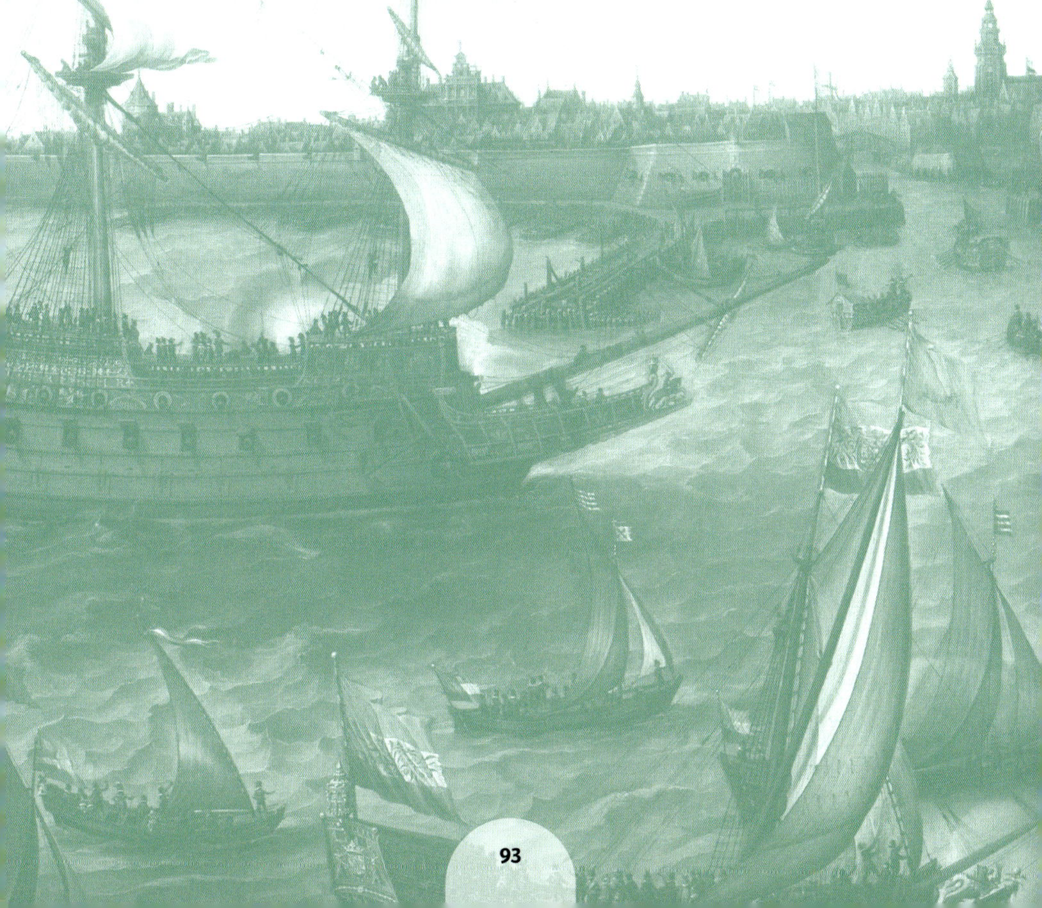

Maarten van Heemskerck
Heemskerk, 1498 – Haarlem, 1574

Saint Luke Painting the Madonna, 1532
oil on panel

According to legend, Saint Luke painted a portrait of the Madonna with the infant Jesus. Luke therefore became the patron saint of artists. We see him at work here, keenly focused on the task at hand. Behind him is Inspiration, who has Van Heemskerck's face. Van Heemskerck painted this piece for the Haarlem Guild of St Luke, the professional association of artists. He presented it to the guild just before he travelled to Italy, in the hope that his fellow artists would pray for him.

Van Heemskerck painted this image on two separate panels, which were later joined. The work was recently restored and separated into its original two parts again.

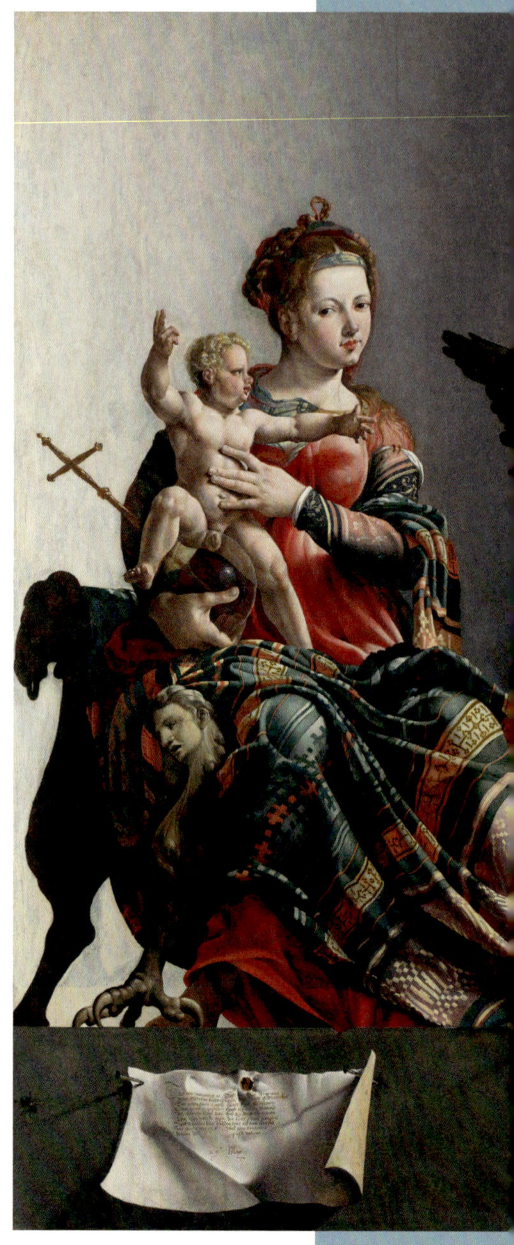

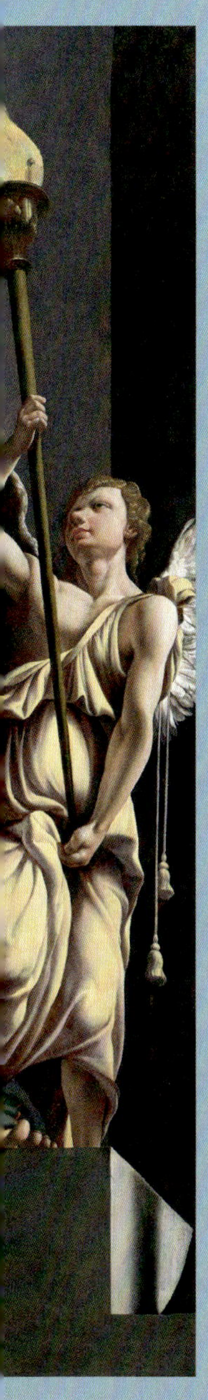

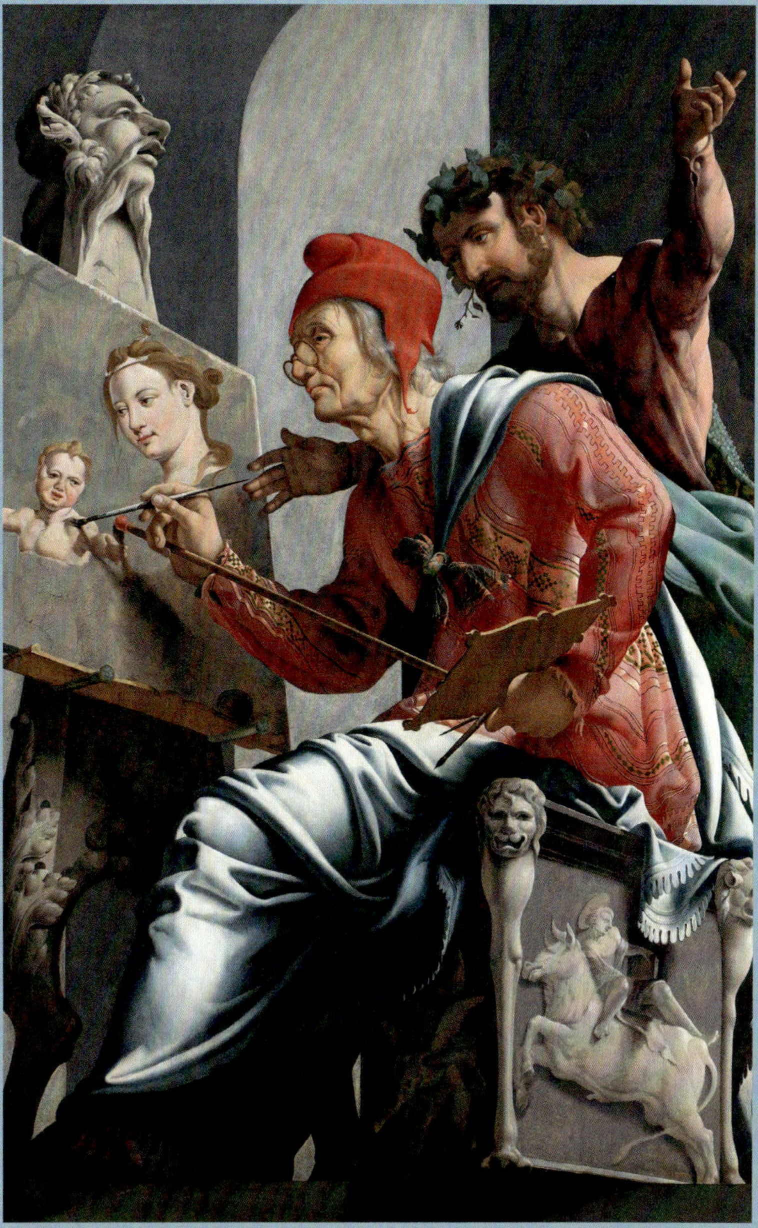

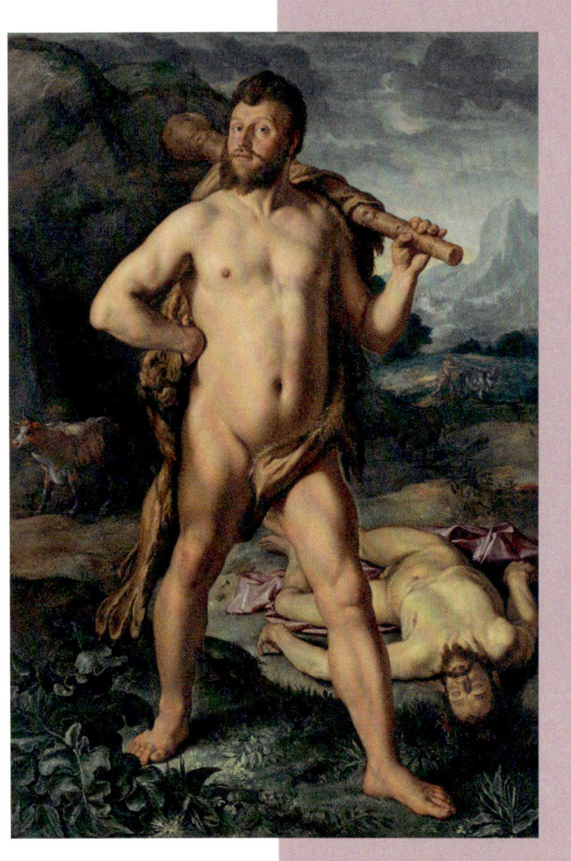

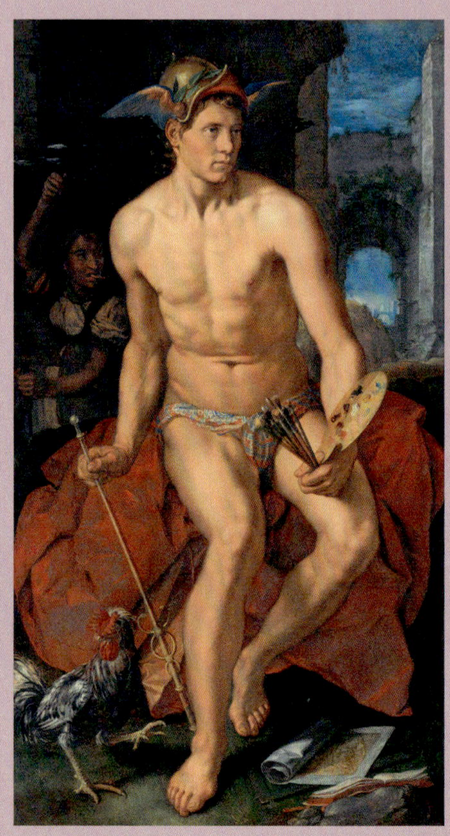

Hendrick Goltzius

Mühlbracht, 1558 – Haarlem, 1617

Hercules and Cacus, 1613
Mercury, 1611
Minerva, 1611

oil on canvas

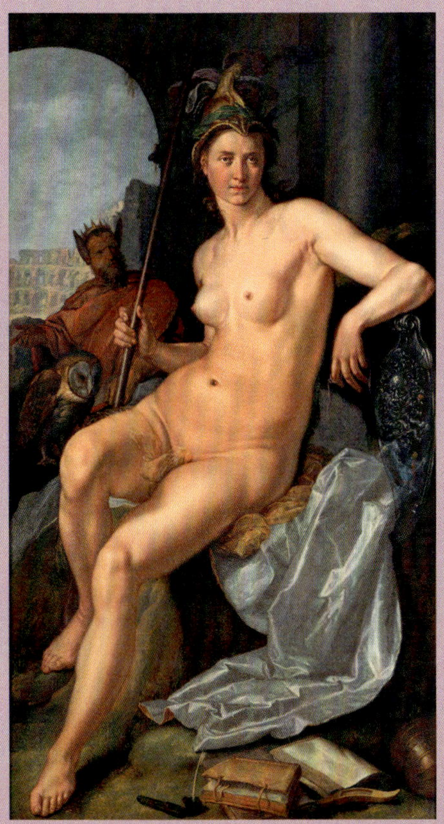

Hendrick Goltzius became familiar with the art of classical antiquity and the Italian Renaissance in Italy. This can be seen in these life-sized images of the Roman gods Mercury and Minerva, with their perfect physiques. Mercury was protector of the arts and of rhetoric, Minerva the goddess of knowledge and war. That is why Goltzius painted a chattering woman behind Mercury, and the foolish King Midas behind Minerva.

Two years later Goltzius painted the classical hero Hercules with the defeated giant Cacus. The painting was commissioned by a Haarlem lawyer, Johan Colterman, who also bought his *Minerva* and *Mercury*. Colterman's son probably modelled for the painting, which explains a lot. Goltzius' Hercules is no son of a god, but clearly a mere mortal.

on loan from the Mauritshuis, The Hague

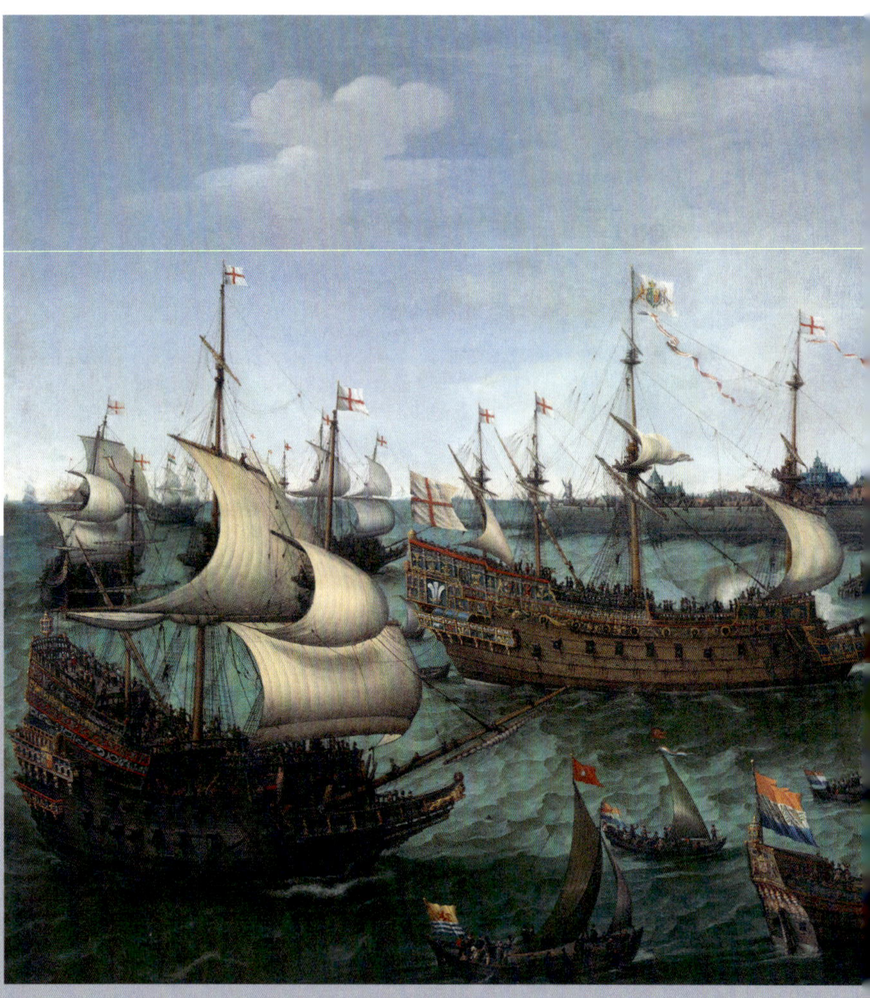

Hendrik Vroom
Haarlem, 1562/63 – Haarlem, 1640

The Arrival of Frederick V of the Palatinate and Elizabeth Stuart in Flushing on 29 April 1613, 1623
oil on canvas

In 1613, Princess Elizabeth Stuart of England and her husband Frederick V, the Elector Palatine, landed at Flushing. They were welcomed by Stadtholder Maurice of Orange, who was related to Frederick. This moment was so important that ten years later Hendrik

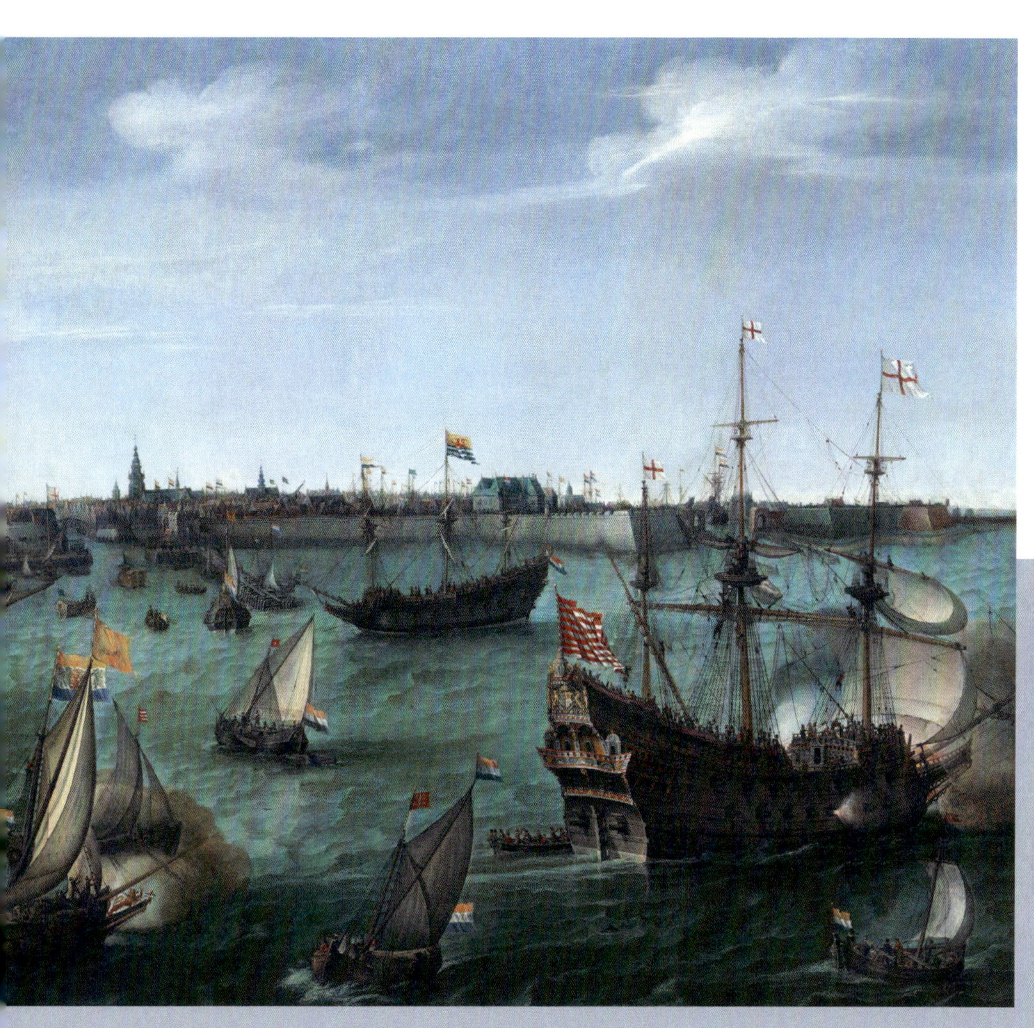

Vroom captured it in this painting. He depicted a festive occasion, with gun salutes, flags flying and ships and boats on the water. As the originator of Dutch seascape painting, Vroom's ability to capture a scene such as this was unparalleled.

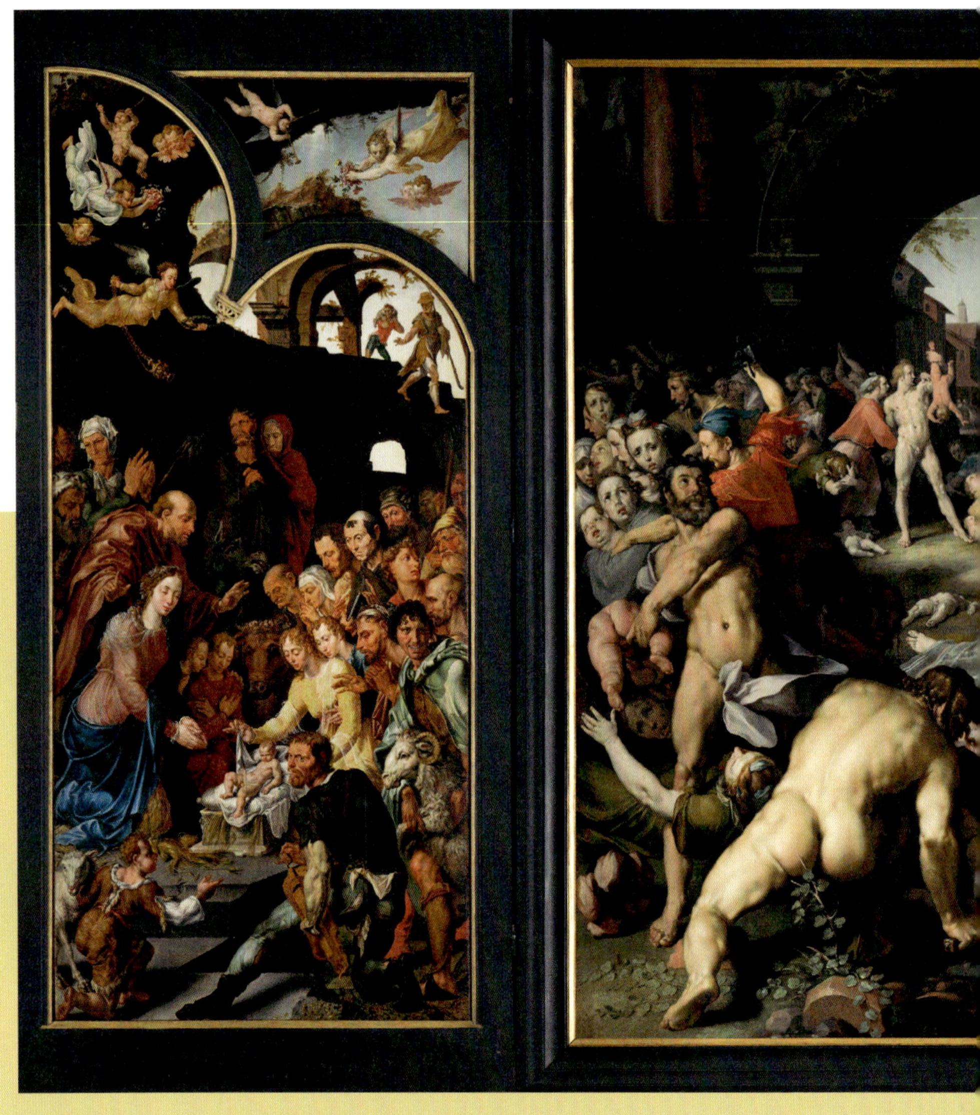

Maarten van Heemskerck
Heemskerk, 1498 – Haarlem, 1574
and Cornelis Cornelisz van Haarlem
Haarlem, 1562 – Haarlem, 1638

Drapers' Altarpiece, 1546/7 and 1591
oil on panel (side panels) and canvas (middle panel)

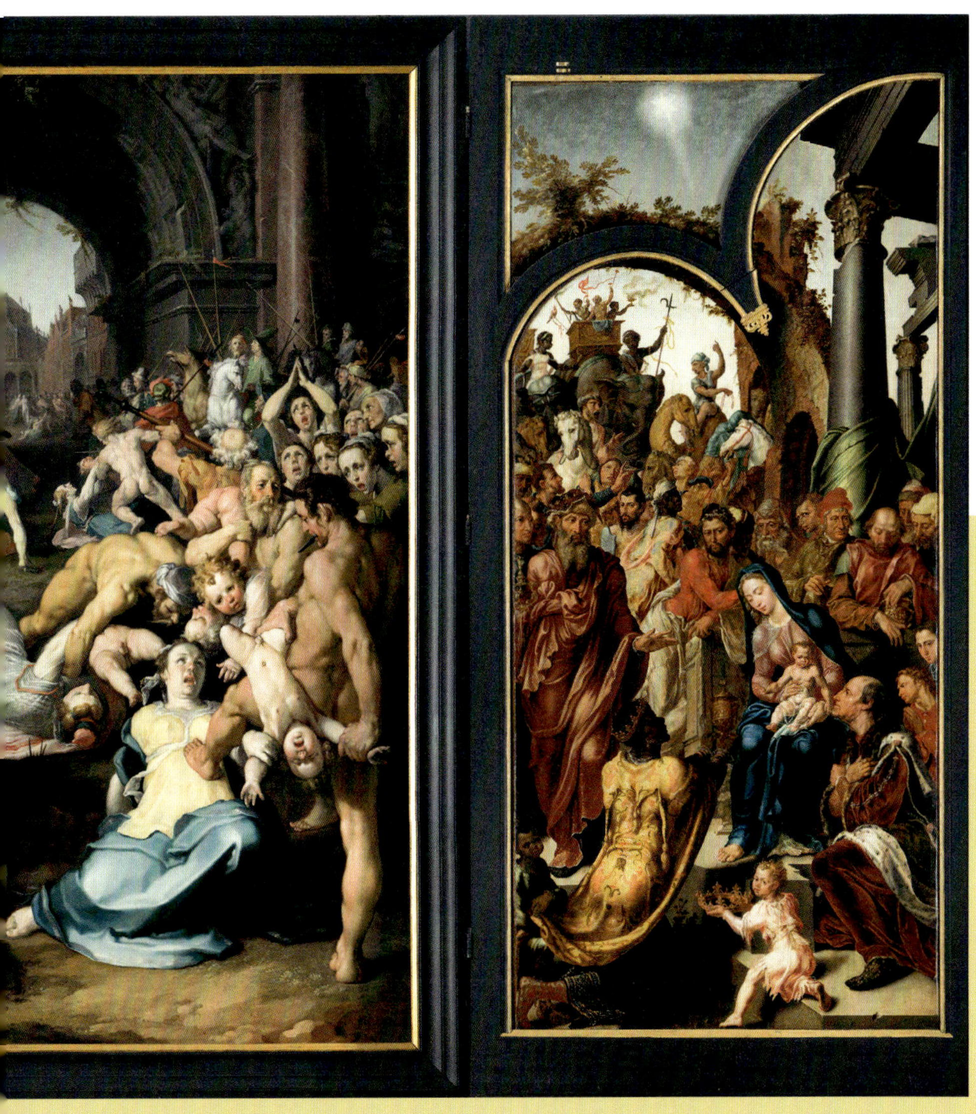

The Haarlem guild of wool weavers and merchants ('drapers') commissioned Maarten van Heemskerck to paint two side panels for an older altarpiece. On the left, he painted the shepherds worshipping the infant Jesus; on the right, the Three Magi.

The original middle panel was lost some thirty years later, and Cornelis van Haarlem was commissioned to paint a replacement. He too depicted an episode from the Christmas story: the gruesome Massacre of the Innocents in Bethlehem.

on loan from the Mauritshuis, The Hague

Cornelis Cornelisz van Haarlem

Haarlem, 1562 – Haarlem, 1638

The Wedding of Peleus and Thetis, 1592/93

oil on canvas

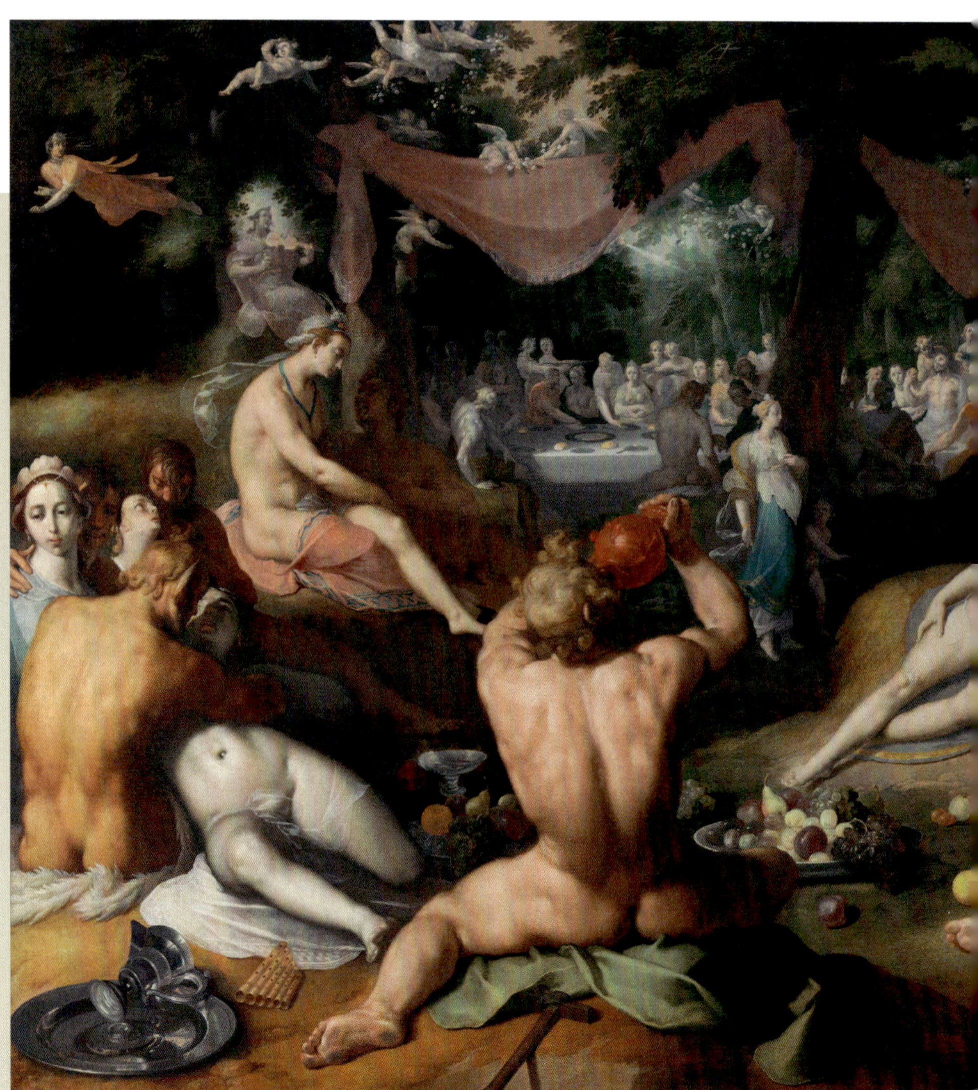

Haarlem town council commissioned Cornelis Cornelisz to produce a painting depicting the wedding of Thetis and Peleus, a story from Greek mythology. Eris, goddess of discord or conflict, was not invited to the wedding, but she came anyway. We see her making her escape on the left, after tossing a golden apple labelled 'for the fairest' among the guests. The apple caused conflict among the gods, which eventually led to the outbreak of the Trojan War. The painting hung in the town's guest accommodation, with a clear message for visitors: avoid conflict, for it can have major consequences.

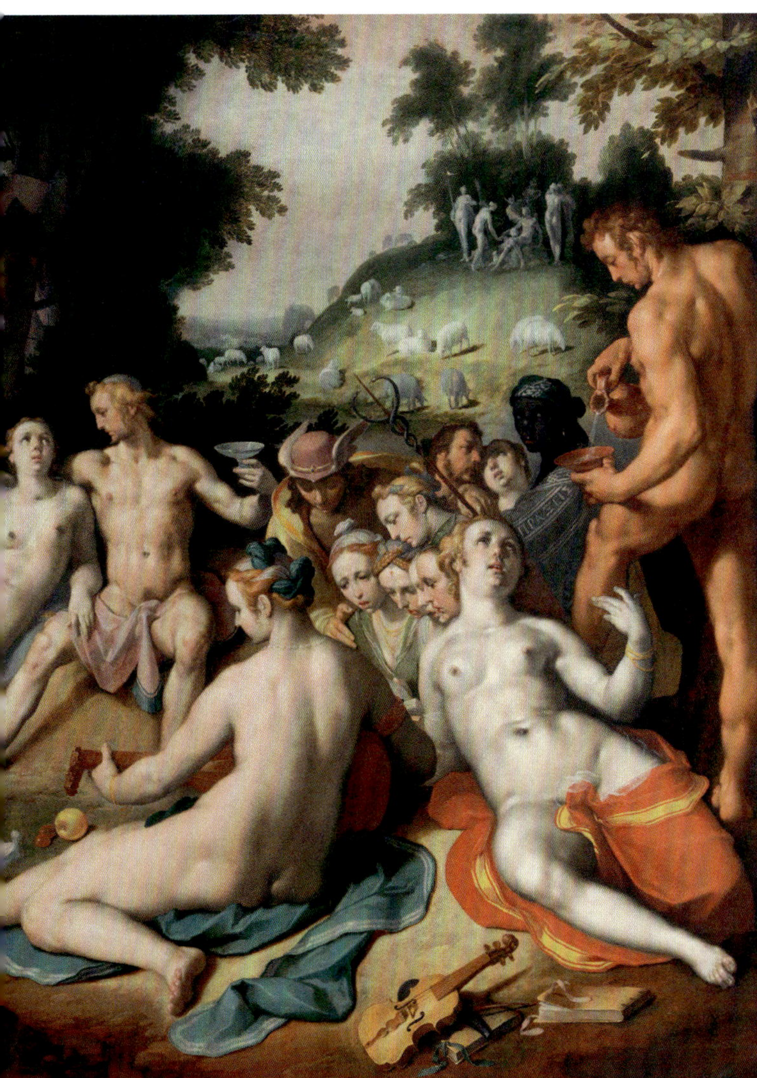

on loan from the Mauritshuis, The Hague

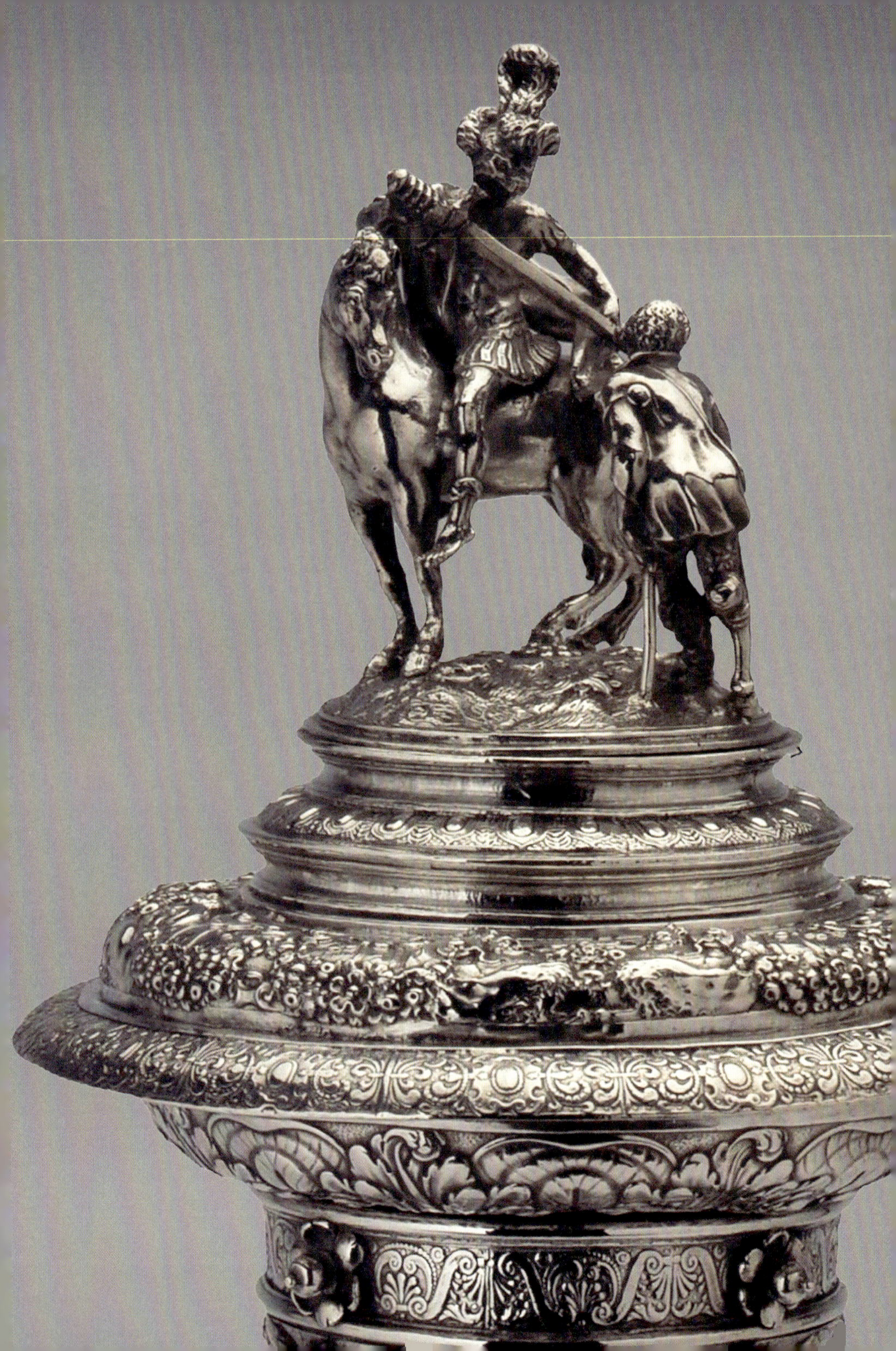

Various Artists

Goblet of the Haarlem Guild of St Martin, 1604/05

silver

The brewers of Haarlem had their own association, the Guild of St Martin. They showed off their wealth by commissioning this superb goblet, which is a masterpiece of silversmithing. Printmaker Hendrick Goltzius and sculptor Hendrick de Keyser produced designs, and silversmiths Ernst van Vianen and Jacob Pietersz van Alckemade made the goblet itself. To remind the brewers that life is not only about money, the goblet is decorated with scenes from the life of Saint Martin, who shared his warm winter cloak with a poor man.

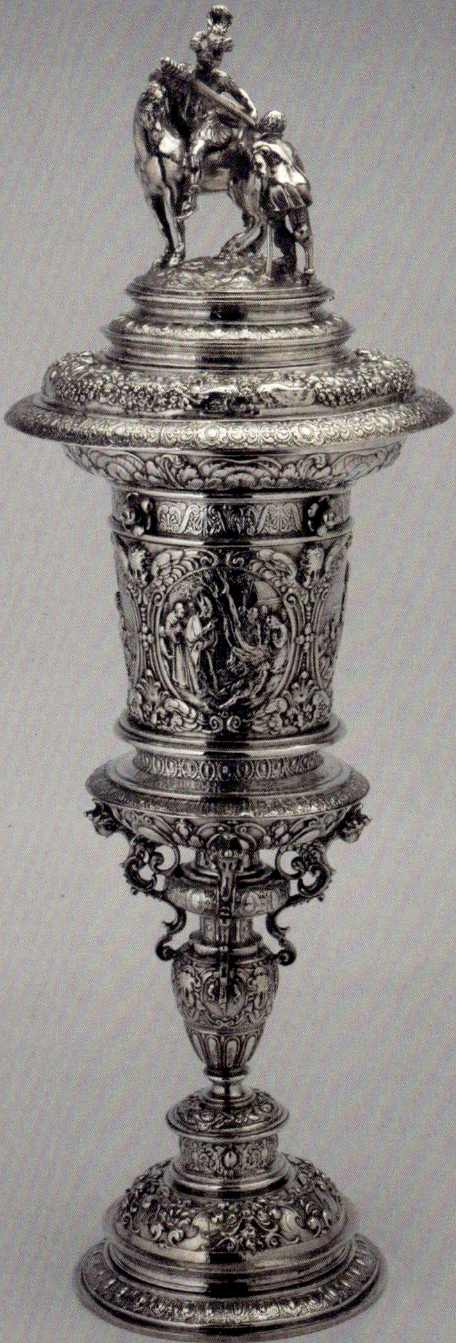

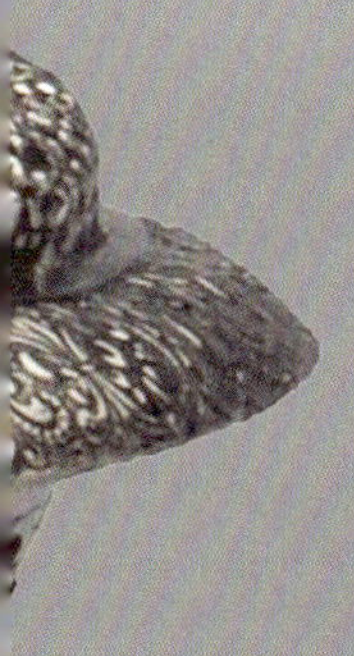

patricia kaersenhout

b. 1966, Den Helder

Guess Who's Coming to Dinner Too, 2017-2019

installation in wood, steel, glass, textile

Seated at a table set for dinner, patricia kaersenhout gives forgotten women a prominent place at the museum, and thus in the history of art. The complete installation consists of four tables, each of which seats fifteen female heroes of the resistance. Black women and women of colour, from all over the world and from different periods. Women who fought various forms of oppression, including colonialism, slavery and the patriarchy. Many of these women deliberately operated outside the existing power structures, and thus remained anonymous, but here they have been given a seat at the table. kaersenhout based her work on Judy Chicago's *The Dinner Party* (1974-1979), an important feminist artwork.

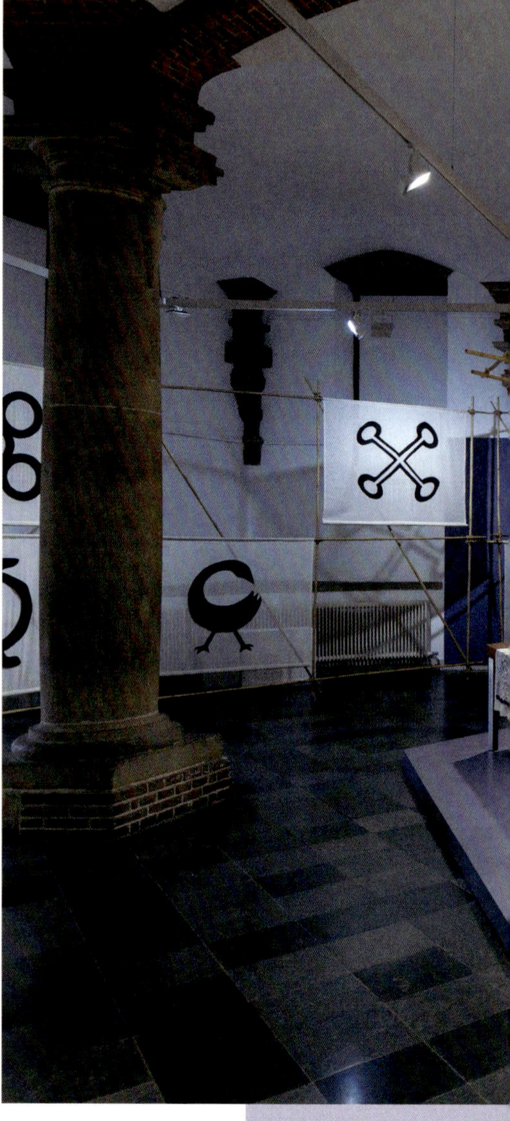

acquired in collaboration with Stedelijk Museum Amsterdam, Centraal Museum Utrecht and Van Abbemuseum Eindhoven, with the support of the Rembrandt Association (courtesy of its Titus Fonds, its Caius Fonds, its Desirée Lambers Fonds and the annual donation from the Cultuurfonds) and the Mondriaan Fund

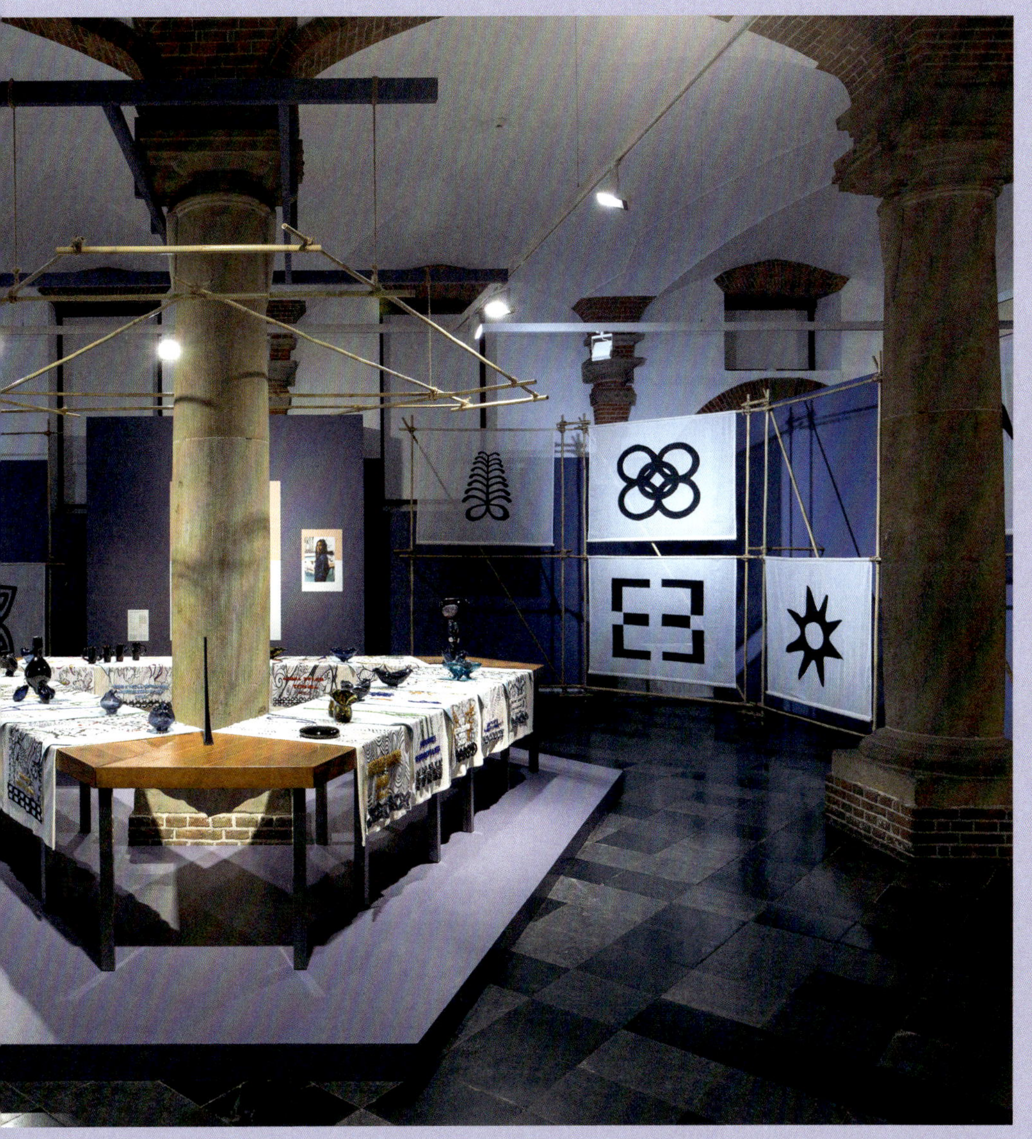

Highlights

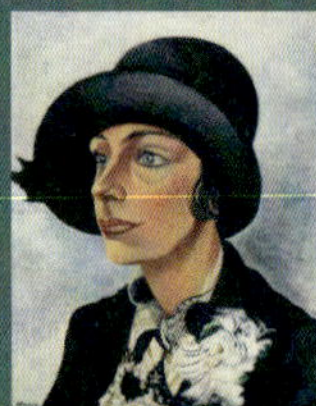

Charley Toorop
Woman in a Black Hat, probably Annie Oud-Dinaux

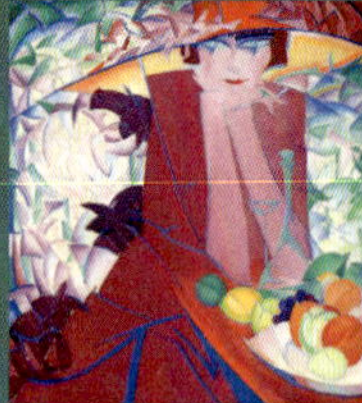

Leo Gestel
Woman in a Large Hat in a Summer House

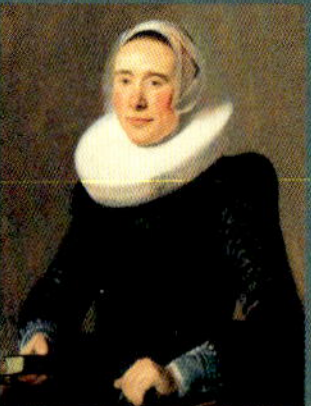

Judith Leyster
Portrait of an Unknown Woman

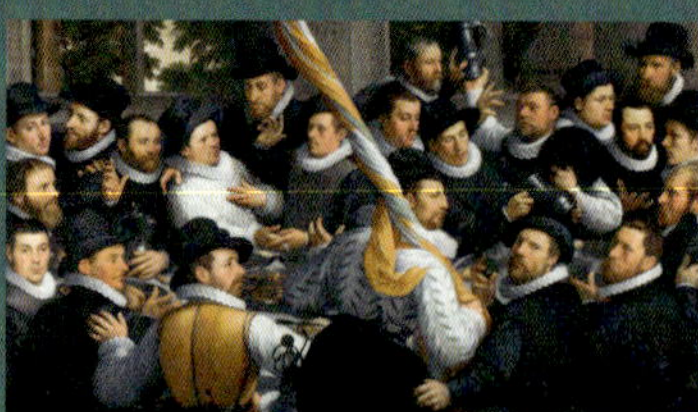

Cornelis Cornelisz van Haarlem
Banquet of Members of the Haarlem Calivermen Civic Guard

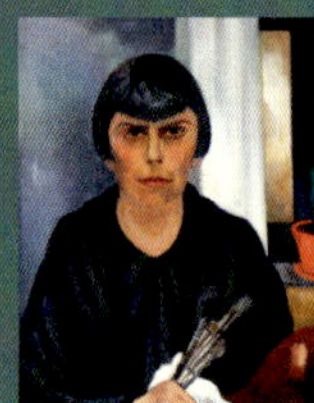

Else Berg
Self-Portrait with Brushes

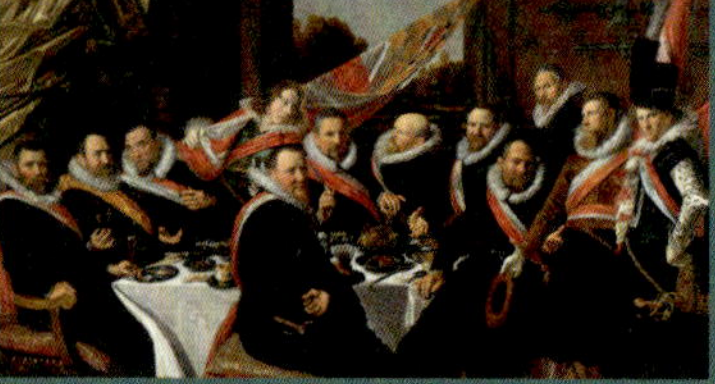

Frans Hals
Banquet of the Officers of St George's Civic Guard

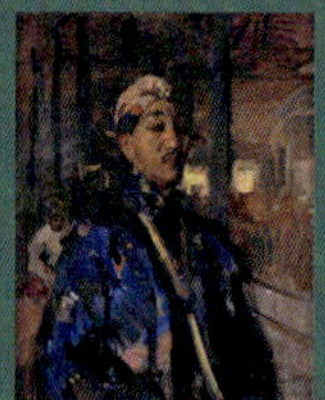

Isaac Israels
Portrait of Mankunegara VII, a Javanese Ruler

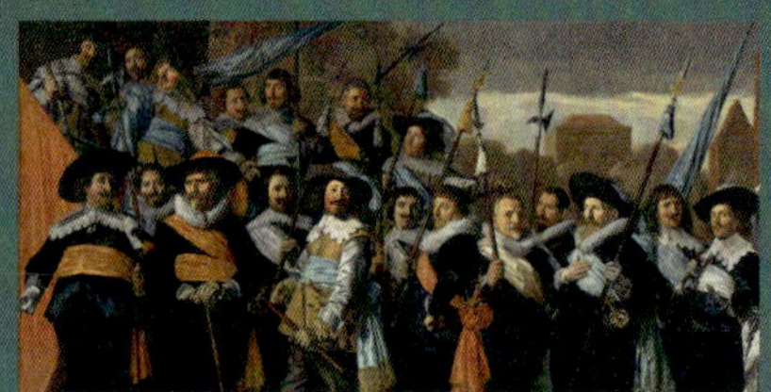

Frans Hals
Officers and Sergeants of St George's Civic Guard

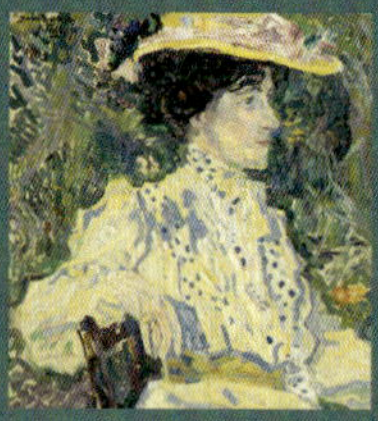

Jan Toorop
Portret van Elisa Beetz-Charpentier

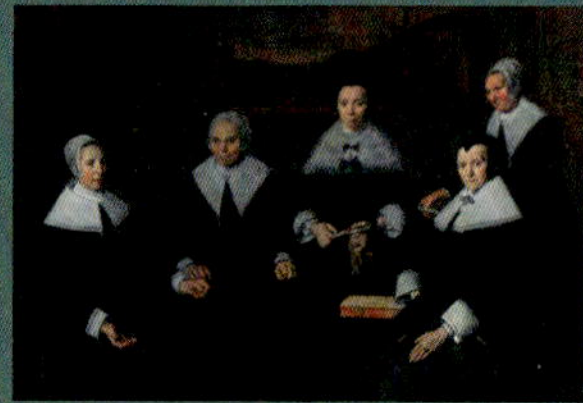

Frans Hals
Regentesses of the Old Men's Almshouse

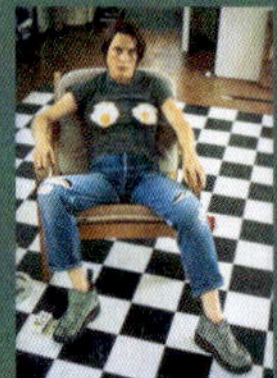

Sarah Lucas
Self-Portrait with Fried Eggs

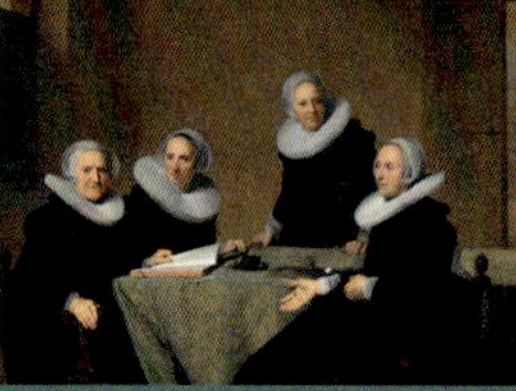

Johannes Cornelisz Verspronck
Regentesses of St Elisabeth's Hospital

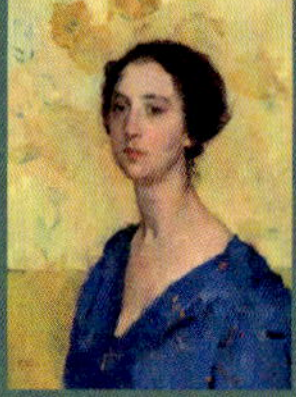

Isaac Israels
Portrait of Rosalie Zélander-Caffé

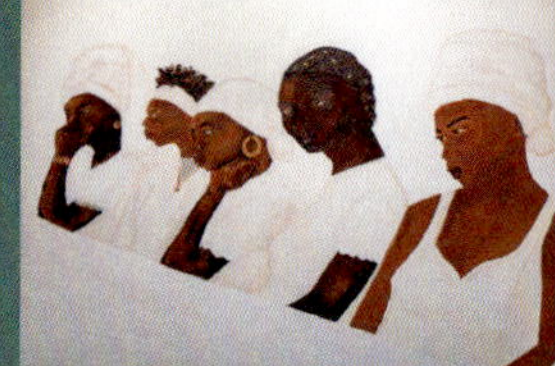

Iriée Zamblé
Wishing on a Star

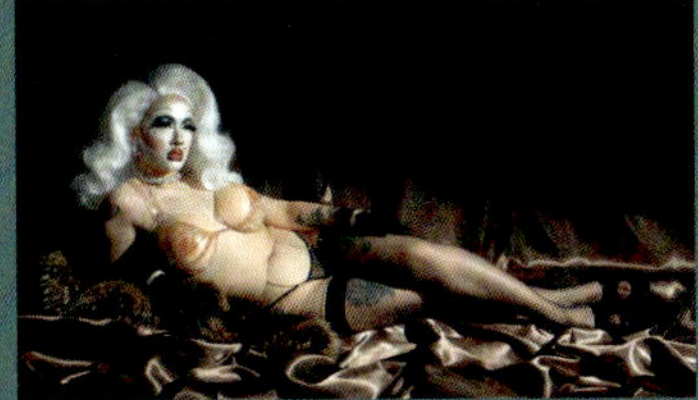

Sin Wai Kin
Act I Part I, Tell me everything you saw, and what you think it means

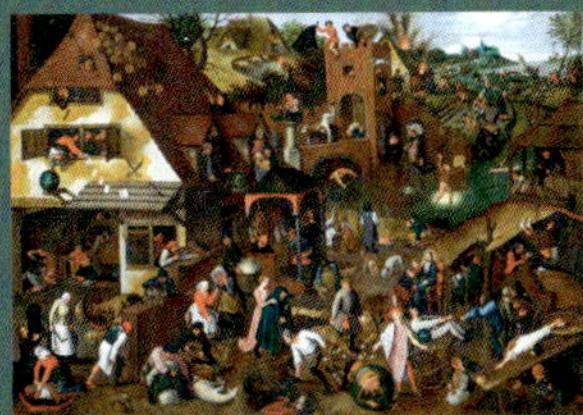

Pieter Brueghel II
Dutch Proverbs

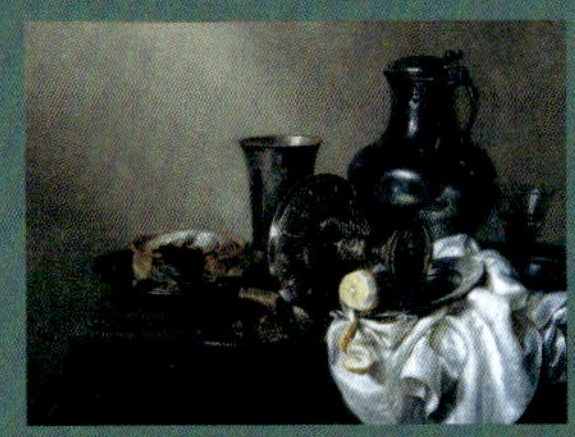

Willem Claesz Heda
Still Life with Half-eaten Pie

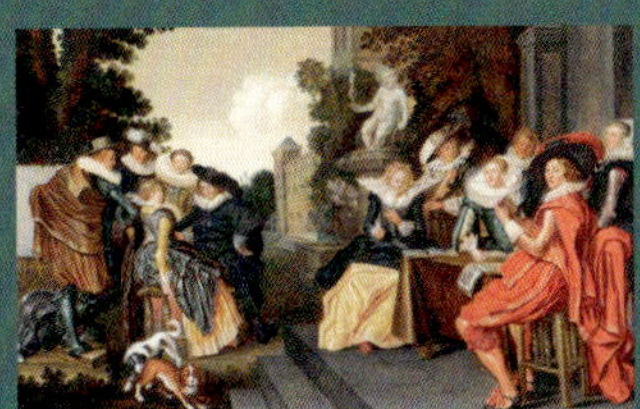

Dirck Hals
Company Playing Music in a Garden

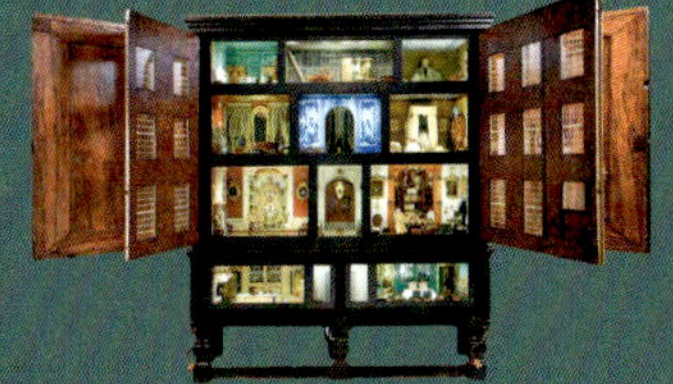

Sara Rothé Doll's House

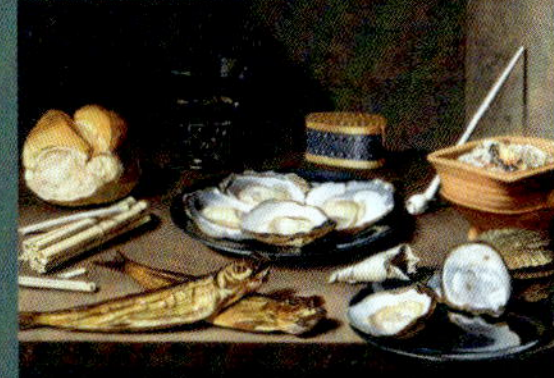

Floris van Schooten
Still Life with Herring, Oysters and Smokes

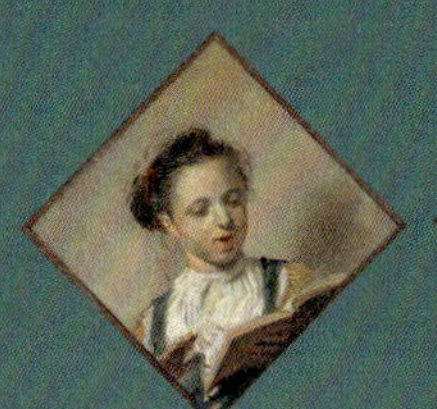

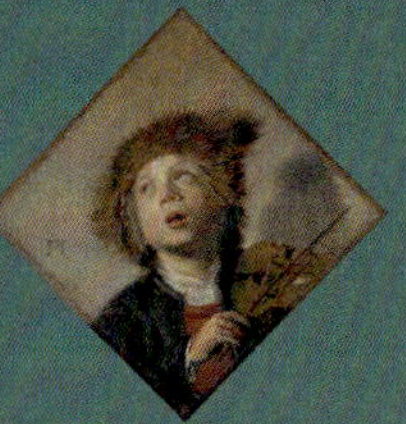

Frans Hals
Singing Girl and Boy Playing the Violin

Ferdinand Erfmann
Bar

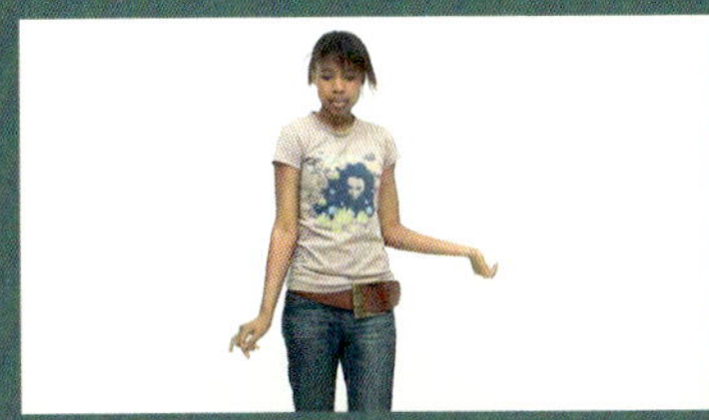

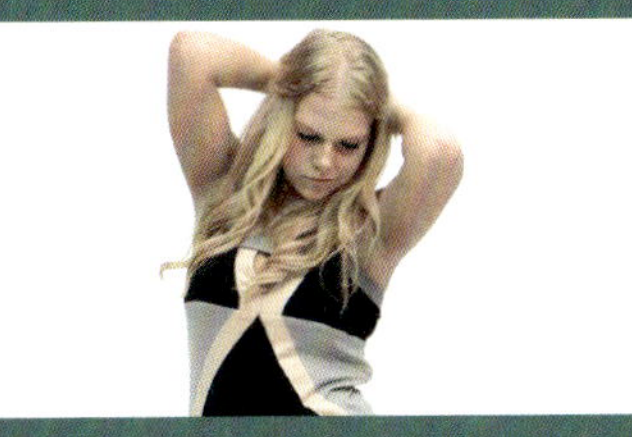

Rineke Dijkstra
The Krazyhouse (Megan, Simon, Nicky, Philip, Dee), Liverpool, UK

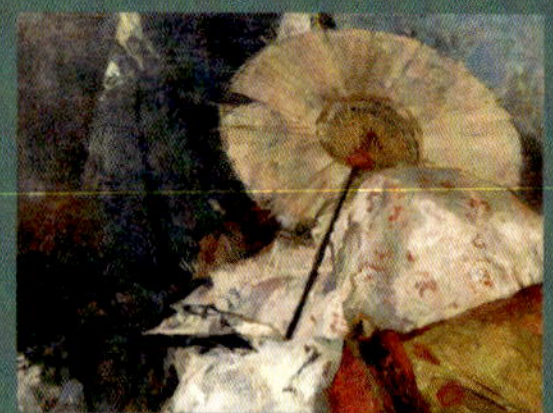

Coba Ritsema
Still Life with Pink Parasol

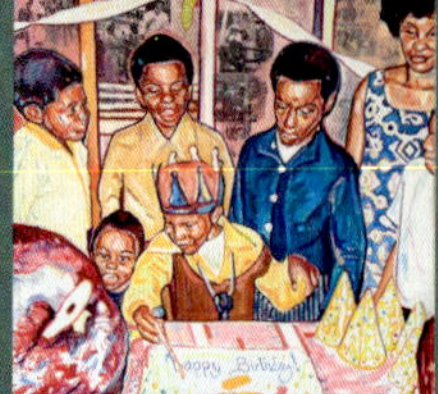

Esiri Erheriene-Essi
Having Your Cake and Eating it Too

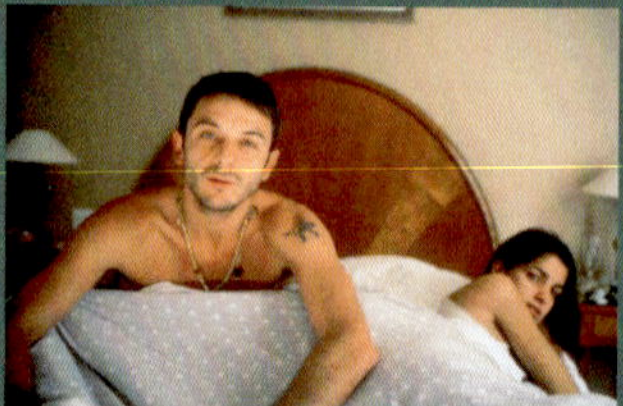

Nan Goldin
Heartbeat

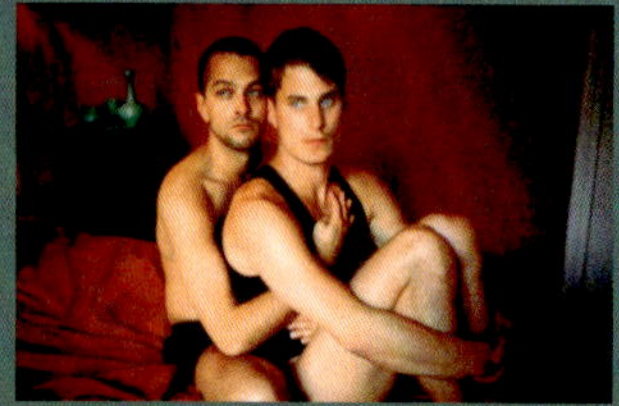

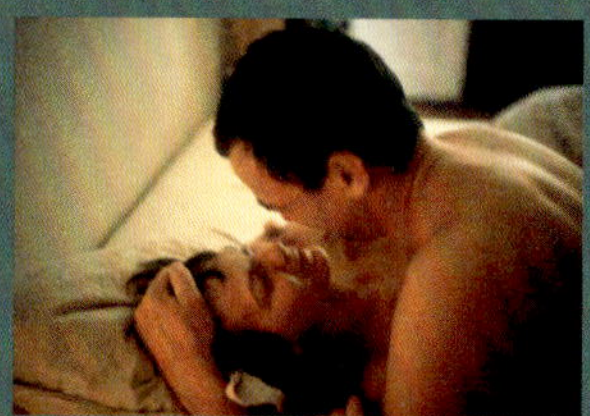

Nan Goldin
Heartbeat

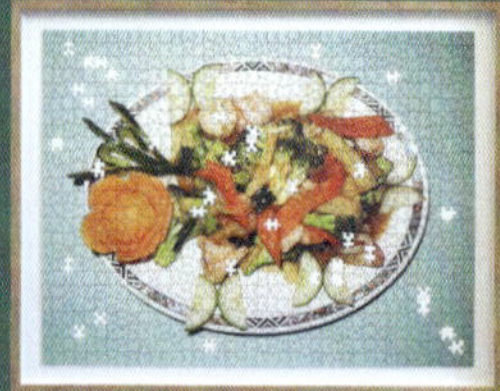

Benjamin Li
No. 85 with Rice – Prawns and Broccoli

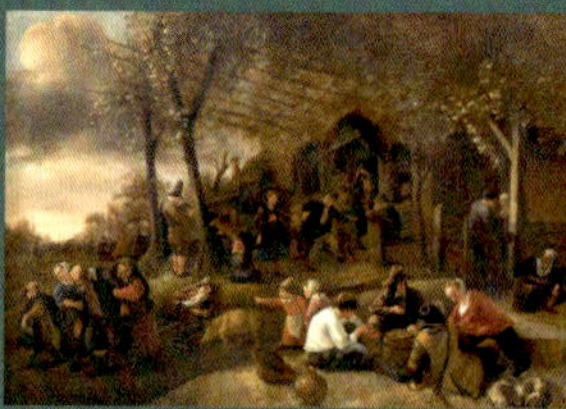

Jan Steen
A Village Fair

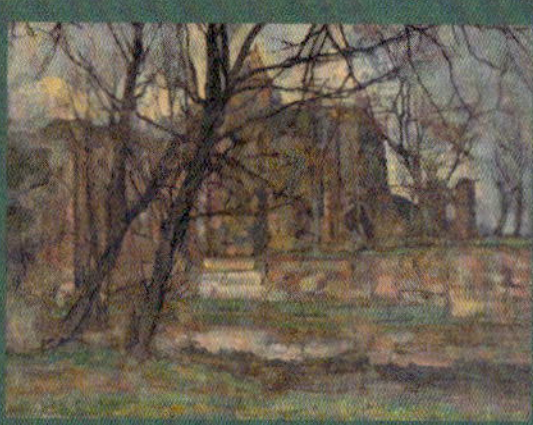

Piet Mondrian
The Ruin of Brederode Castle

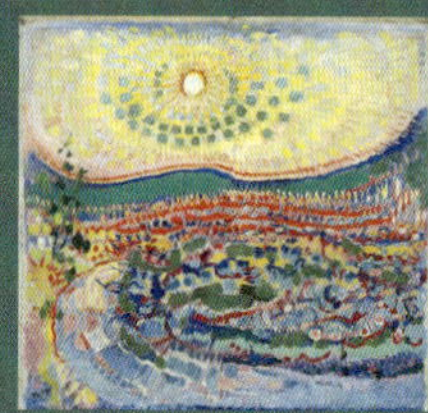

Jan Sluijters
October Sun, Laren

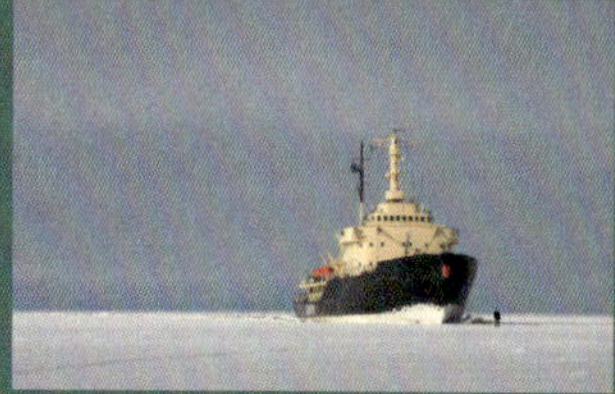

Guido van der Werve
Number eight, everything is going to be alright

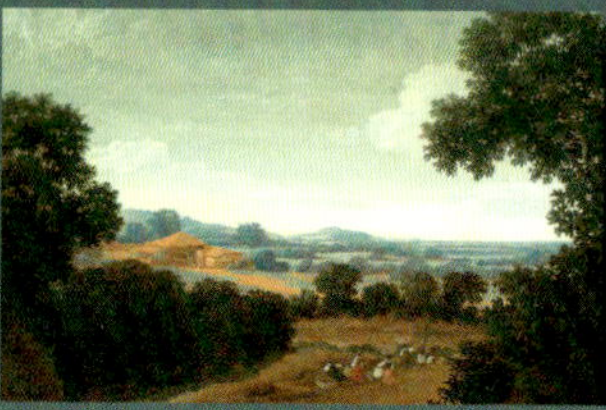

Frans Post
Brazilian Landscape

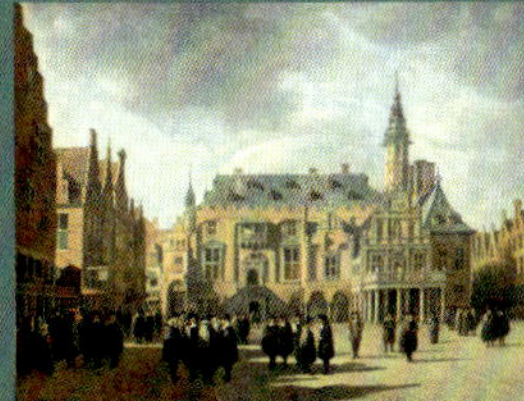

Gerrit Berckheyde
Grote Markt with the Town Hall

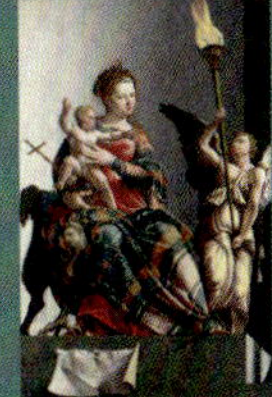

Maarten van Heemskerck
Saint Luke Painting the Madonna

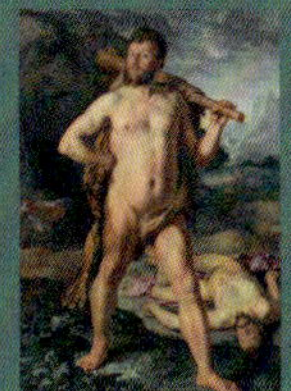

Hendrick Goltzius
Hercules and Cacus

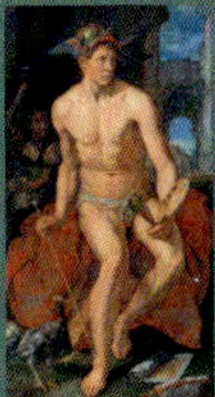

Mercury

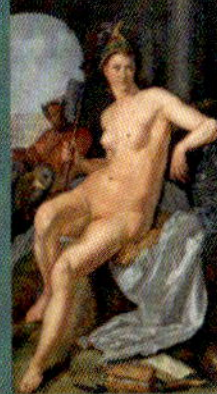

Minerva

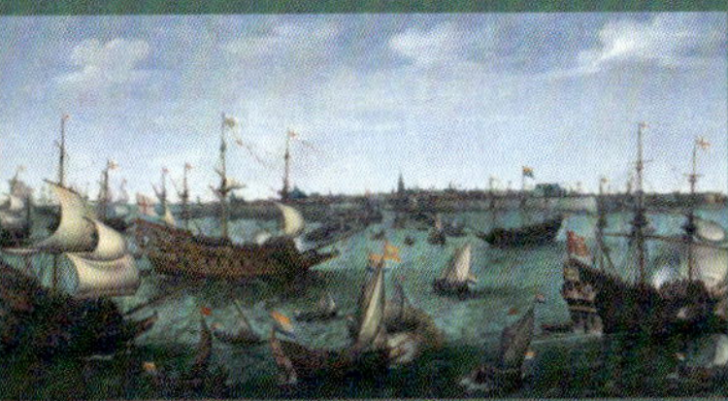

Hendrik Vroom
The Arrival of Frederick V of the Palatinate and Elizabeth Stuart in Flushing on 29 April 1613

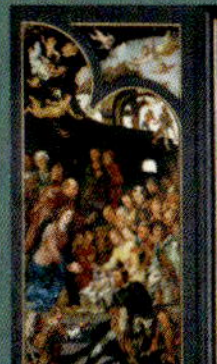

Maarten van Heemskerck and Cornelis Cornelisz van Haarlem
Drapers' Altarpiece

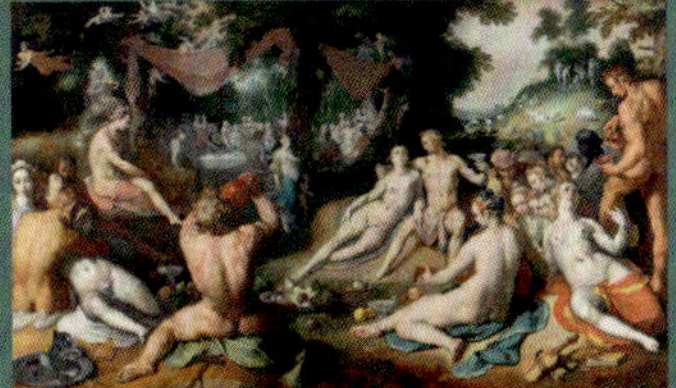

Cornelis Cornelisz van Haarlem
The Wedding of Peleus and Thetis

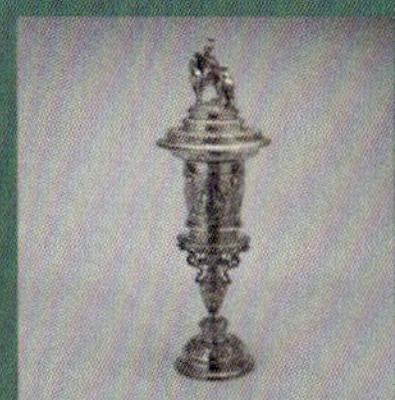

Various Artists
Goblet of the Haarlem Guild of St Martin

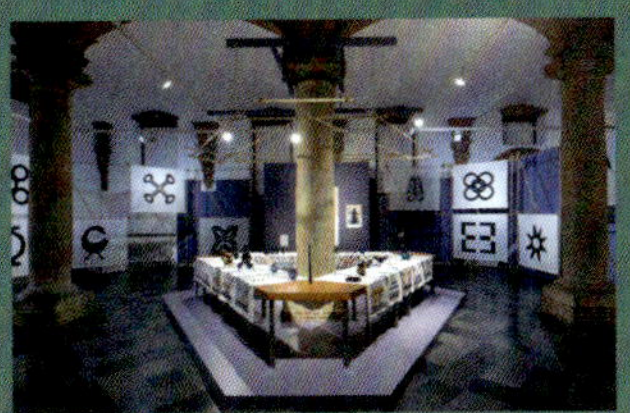

patricia kaersenhout
Guess Who's Coming to Dinner Too

publication
Frans Hals Museum, Haarlem
Waanders Publishers, Zwolle

content
Christi Klinkert (senior curator of old masters)
Maaike Rikhof (curator of modern art)
Manique Hendricks (curator of contemporary art)
Karlien Dijkstra (senior educator)
Paul Stork (business director)
Geert-Jan Borgstein (editor)

translation
Sue McDonnell

design
Frank de Wit

lithography
Benno Slijkhuis, Wilco Art Books

printing
Wilco Art Books, Amersfoort

photography
René Gerritsen Kunst & Onderzoeksfotografie 16-17, 28-29, 44-45, 94-95, 96-97, 102-103
Tom Haartsen 10-11, 20-21, 24-25, 26-27, 46-47, 48-49, 52-53, 58-59, 78-79, 84-85, 86-87, 98-99, 104-105
Doro Keman 80-81
Fabian Landewee 36-37
Charlott Markus 106-107
Margareta Svensson 14-15, 32-33, 50-51, 100-101
Arend Velsink 12-13, 18-19, 30-31, 34-35, 56-57, 60-61, 88-89
Virginia Museum of Fine Arts 54-55
Thijs Quispel 22-23, 82-83

ISBN 9789462626829
A Dutch edition is also available
(ISBN 9789462626812)
NUR 643

franshalsmuseum.nl
waanders.nl

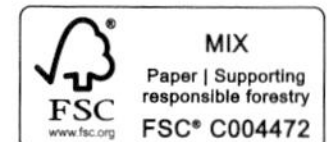